Embracing Eternity

IN THE HERE AND NOW

How the book of Ecclesiastes helps us live more peaceful, purposeful, and plentiful lives today.

LAURA R BAILEY

Copyright © 2024 Laura R Bailey

All rights reserved. No part of this book may be used or reproduced by any means, graphic, electronic, or mechanical, including photocopying, recording, taping, or by any information storage retrieval system without the written permission of the publisher, except in the case of brief quotations embodied in critical articles and reviews.

Unless otherwise noted, Scripture is taken from the Holy Bible, NEW INTERNATIONAL VERSION ® Copyright © 1973, 1978, 1984 by Biblica, INC. All rights reserved worldwide. Used by permission. NEW INTERNATIONAL VERSION ® and NIV ® are registered trademarks of Biblica, INC. Use of either trademark for the offering of goods or services requires the prior written consent of Biblica US, Inc. Because of the dynamic nature of the internet, any web addresses or links contained in this book may have changed since publication and may no longer be valid.

Editor: Megan Conner

Author photo by : The Zigs Creative

Formatted by Jen Henderson at Wild Words Formatting

Cover: Angie Alaya

LauraRBailey.com

PRAISE FOR
Embracing Eternity
IN THE HERE AND NOW

"Join Laura as she walks us through contemplative Ecclesiastes, gently inviting us to shift our gaze from the emptiness of our hustle to the full, abundant life found in Jesus. She guides us through one of the most philosophical books of the Bible a few verses at a time, diving below the surface to unearth contextual meaning and relating it to our everyday lives. More importantly, Laura daily inspires us to do the "hard heart work" that leads to real-life change. Each devotion ends with a prayer prompt to posture your heart in worship of God. *Embracing Eternity in the Here and Now* is an encouraging, theologically grounded devotional perfect for the woman looking for purpose, meaning and life beyond her never-ending to-do list."

Shelby Dixon, Encouragement for Today Devotions Manager at Proverbs 31 Ministries

"Do you ever feel like your life is meaningless? You hustle and wear yourself out doing all the right things for everyone and to what end? If you are longing for peace and purpose in this life and in the next, *Embracing Eternity in the Here and Now* is for you. In these pages, Laura Bailey empathizes with your struggle and guides you through the book of Ecclesiastes to impart Solomon's wisdom to apply to your own life. You can live in light of eternity now. This devotional will show you how."

Rachael Adams, author of *A Little Goes a Long Way* and *Everyday Prayers for Love*

"*Embracing Eternity in the Here and Now* is a relatable, biblically sound devotional that feels like you're being led through the book of Ecclesiastes by a trusted friend. Laura does a wonderful job of helping us understand this ancient text through the lens of our current circumstances, sharing her stories and experiences with transparency and love. Whether you've read Ecclesiastes before or you're new to this book, *Embracing Eternity in the Here and Now* will equip and encourage you in your walk with the Lord."

Mandy Johnson, Writer and Speaker
@ www.mandycjohnson.com

"The demands of each day gets us swirling in a sea of the next emergency assaulting us. *Embracing Eternity* sets our hearts and minds each new day in the direction on what is eternal. The unexpected benefits we gain is a release from anxiety about this day in front of us and hope in Father's promise of a purpose anchored in Himself."

Lynn Cowell, author of *Fearless Women of the Bible*
and *Esther: Seeing an Invisible God in an Uncertain World*

For my Nana, Jean Register Dickens

Her obedience to the Lord, faithfulness in prayer, dedication to serving others, and personal relationship with Jesus, left a legacy that pointed to Christ. I am truly grateful for the time I had with her on earth, and look forward to worshiping our Savior with her in eternity.

"He has made everything beautiful in its time. He has also set eternity in the human heart; yet no one can fathom what God has done from beginning to end."
Ecclesiastes 3:11

WHEN WE LIVE WITH THE *Eternal* IN MIND, IT INFORMS HOW WE LIVE *Today.*

Introduction: Tired of Pretending	1
How to Read This Book	7
Day 1: Live Each Day Like It's Your Last	10
Day 2: What Is the Point of All Our Busyness?	15
Day 3: The Search for Meaning	20
Day 4: Take the Vacation but Monday Is Coming	24
Day 5: Not All Things Are Worth Knowing	29
Day 6: Work to Live, Not Live to Work	34
Day 7: Nothing Lasts Forever	39
Day 8: Keeping Our Bags Packed	43
Day 9: Life Isn't Fair	47
Day 10: People Need People	52
Day 11: The Dangers of a Checklist Christianity	57
Day 12: Money Can't Buy Lasting Happiness	62
Day 13: Money Won't Buy You Everything	68
Day 14: How Will Your Life Be Remembered?	74
Day 15: Serenity to Accept the Things We Cannot Change	79
Day 16: Submission Even When It's Hard	85
Day 17: Embracing Each Day as a Gift	91
Day 18: Trusting God When It Doesn't Make Sense	98
Day 19: Flourishing in the Waiting	104
Day 20: There May Not Always Be Tomorrow	110
Day 21: How to Not Waste Your Life	116
Eternal Wanderlust	123
About the Author	127
Teaching Ministry	129
Connect with Laura	131

WE ARE *Eternal* BEINGS. WHEN WE TRY TO FILL OUR LIVES WITH *Temporary* THINGS, IT WILL ALWAYS LEAVE US LONGING FOR *More.*

Introduction
TIRED OF PRETENDING

"I don't know if I can do this anymore. I need to go home."

Through uncontrollable sobs, I asked my boss if I could take the rest of the day off. So taken aback by my uncharacteristic show of emotion, he didn't ask any questions.

He simply said, " Sure, whatever you need."

I raced home, dropped to my knees, and cried to God, "I'm done doing things my way. I am tired of running, playing games, and pretending. I surrender my whole life over to You."

I was utterly exhausted. At the literal end of my rope, my joy for life was completely drained. I was like the duck who, on the surface, glides along smoothly without a care in the world, but underneath the water, is paddling like crazy just to stay afloat, one kick shy of drowning completely.

From the outside looking in, I was living the American dream. I had a successful career in my late twenties, was married, and had purchased my first home. My social calendar overflowed with sporting events, getaways, and gatherings with friends. My life checked all the right boxes. I should have been satisfied.

Yet, I was miserable.

I was plagued with anxiety over potentially losing my position at the top. Unable to sleep, most days, I struggled to get out of bed. In an attempt to calm my racing thoughts and temper my constant mood swings, I tried medication, fad diets, and the latest craze that promised a continuous state of euphoria. My weekends were spent yo-yo-ing between extremes: overindulgence or complete slothfulness, hoping to numb and avoid my feeling of emptiness.

The bigger the commission check, the more I wanted. There was no time to celebrate my success. My relationships were surface-level at best. I only made time for people who could help advance my career or social status. Loneliness and inadequacy took up permanent residence in my heart, and no matter what I tried, like unwelcome house guests, they would not leave.

I was doing everything that was supposed to make me happy. Why, then, did I feel empty inside? Why did nothing satisfy the constant ache in my heart? Not my job, my dress size, or social events. Not even my relationship with my husband could soothe the unceasing angst. Nothing left me satiated for long. In most cases, my attempts at buying happiness only made me feel more deficient. The irony was that I had understood the otherworldly solution since the age of seven. I'd accepted Christ as Savior, but never truly surrendered and submitted my life to Him.

For years, I believed countless lies about how to find lasting contentment, what it meant to be successful, and how to make your life count. However, I was too blinded by the flashing lights of this reality. As I found out, all that glitters is not gold.

Until one day, my life changed.

INTRODUCTION

THE MEETING THAT CHANGED MY LIFE

I was at lunch with a client and he suddenly paused while sharing about his upcoming order. He looked directly at me and asked, "Laura, how do you know you are a Christian?"

We had talked about our faith before; being in the South, practically everyone attends church. But he had never asked about my spiritual health before. This was completely unexpected.

"How do you see God at work in your life?" he continued.

I didn't even try to hide my annoyance. When the meal ended, I requested the check, waved a quick goodbye, and bolted to my car. What had just happened? Of course, I was saved! I say and do all the right things. If I was so confident in my faith, why then was I so bothered by his question? Why did I feel like something wasn't quite right?

The hard truth was, I really wasn't so sure. I'd been wrestling with God for years. I desperately tried to outrun Him numerous times— going away to college, moving to another country, and immersing myself in work, all so I wouldn't have to deal with my inner conflict. But in the quiet of the night, I would lay awake, anxious, gripped by worry and fear, unable to ignore the constant tug on my heart.

After I drove straight home, I fell to my knees, got down on my face, and prayed, " I surrender. I need help, the help that only You, Lord, can provide."

I was tired of running, trying to appear put together, and believing the lie that my way was better than God's way.

Embracing Eternity IN THE HERE AND NOW

My life visibly changed when I truly surrendered to the Lord. Now, I was not just paying lip service to faith but embracing a genuine heart's desire to serve God and be obedient to His will. The persistent noise in my head gradually diminished as I began to look at life through the lens of eternity. The tantalizing little voice that accused me as I ran from God faded into the background. It was replaced with a sense of peace. I was now a child of God.

Ten years have passed since that lunch meeting, and my life's direction has undoubtedly changed. While obedience to the Lord's call on my life meant walking away from my career, that's not His will for everyone. That's why we must prayerfully ask the Lord to allow us to be open to what He desires for our lives. Every day, we have a choice: live for this world or the next. But it was when I shifted my perspective and started living for eternity, I learned to let go of things that have no lasting significance and cling to what mattered.

A SHIFT IN PERSPECTIVE

For many Christian women, our struggles stem from our loss of proper perspective. We have lost sight of the greater, eternal treasures to be stored up during our time on this earth and have become distracted by lesser, worldly imitations that fail to fill an insatiable void. The enemy seeks to derail us from living eternity-minded at every turn. He whispers convincingly, just as he did in the Garden of Eden, that we deserve to be happy today, no matter what it costs us tomorrow. He wants us to believe that this life is as good as it gets and delights in our pursuit of the next trending allurement. Satan knows that by ignoring the Lord's design for His creation, we miss out on our only source of true peace and lasting contentment.

INTRODUCTION

LIVING FOR ETERNITY

When seeking to understand our temporary residence here on earth and the importance of storing up eternal treasures, the book of Ecclesiastes offers sage wisdom. Reflecting on his very full life, King Solomon observed that things of this world are "meaningless, a chasing after the wind" (Ecclesiastes 1:14). For some readers, Ecclesiastes evokes feelings of gloom and doom, but beware of dismissing Solomon's words as the depressing rant of a frustrated man. Instead, allow them to rouse within you a desire to know God's heart, to trust His purpose for creating us, and to follow His plan for our lives.

Like Solomon, we may find pleasure in financial security, job titles, or a beautiful family and home, but they will never wholly satisfy our longing for more. Anything other than an intimate relationship with our Heavenly Father will leave us dissatisfied, discontent, and disappointed. The inner void we desperately seek can only be filled by Christ alone.

If you have found yourself believing the lie of, "If I just had this," or "If I just get to this point," or " just one more time, then I'll slow down," you've come to the right place. This devotional is for the woman who is exhausted in every way but can't seem to break the cycle of, "If I just," If this is you, know you are good company. We have all learned through numerous, failed attempts that we cannot change our hearts and minds through self-sufficiency. But, there is hope. God has not abandoned us. He is not surprised by our cyclical circumstances. He is ready and waiting for us to invite Him into our hearts and our processes. He is the Prince of Peace and if we yield our wills and our ways to Him, He is faithful to fill every void and calm our anxious hearts.

If this is your desire, let us set out together to shift our perspectives from temporal (sight-based) to eternal (faith-based). God's promises are true. The Lord wants more for His Children. He came so that we could have life and have it to the fullest (John 10:10). Living for eternity doesn't mean we are guaranteed temporal ease and physical comfort. Still, we can cling to our Savior's eternal hope and everlasting promises as we live more peaceful, purposeful, and plentiful lives today.

How to READ THIS BOOK

This book consists of 21 daily readings, covering the entire book of Ecclesiastes. This book was written for you, a woman who already has a full plate and is doing her best to juggle everything. I don't want you to feel this is "just one more thing" on your never-ending to-do list. So friend, if you need to start and stop multiple times in the day, do. If it takes you more than 21 days to read through the pages, that's okay. Set the pace that's right for you.

My hope is that somewhere in your schedule, you can carve out time to spend about 10-15 minutes reading the Scripture and devotional entry. Each day will begin with scripture and then include the following sections:

What does It Mean?
Why Does It Matter?
The Hard Heart Work
Prayer Prompt

Ecclesiastes is a profound book. This devotional only scratches the surface to keep the time commitment manageable. While you will read Ecclesiastes in its entirety, each day focuses on a single main takeaway. If you have extra time or interest to delve deeper, look to a study bible, consult a commentary, or listen to a podcast discussing the book.

I have written a companion 10-Week Bible Study on Ecclesiastes for those interested, to be notified of its release, as well as receive free resources on how to keep an eternal perspective, scan below to learn more.

I am praying for you and cheering you on. It may take a bit of hard heart work, but we can do it! Let's shake off the lesser things and start living more peaceful, purposeful, and plentiful lives today!

AUTHOR NOTE: The writer of Ecclesiastes has been highly debated, but many theologians agree that Solomon is the author. Through personal study, I also agree that Solomon is the teacher found in the pages of Ecclesiastes, and I will reference him as such throughout the devotion.

GOD IS BOTH THE AUTHOR OF LIFE ON *Earth* AND *Eternity.* HE DESIRES HIS CHILDREN TO FIND *Enjoyment* IN BOTH.

Day 1
LIVE EACH DAY LIKE IT'S YOUR LAST

READ: Ecclesiastes 1:1-4

> [1] The words of the Teacher, son of David, king in Jerusalem:
>
> [2] "Meaningless! Meaningless!"
> says the Teacher.
> "Utterly meaningless!
> Everything is meaningless."
>
> [3] What do people gain from all their labors
> at which they toil under the sun?
>
> [4] Generations come and generations go,
> but the earth remains forever.

This year, all three of my girls were enrolled in school for six hours, five days a week. For the first time in a long while, I had an uninterrupted period to work. I am decent at time management, yet every day when the clock struck 2:00 p.m., reminding me it was time to get my girls, I'd ask, "Where did the time go?"

Most days, I can easily attribute the passing hours to my part-time job, volunteering, or other household duties. But there have been many moments, as I drove towards the pick-up line, when I wondered if I had used my time wisely that day. Had I prioritized things that truly matter, or had I filled my day with fluff; checking off items on my to-do list that seemed important, but had no lasting significance?

We are all pulled in numerous directions each and every day. The opportunities for us to invest our time and talents are abundant. How do we make the best choice when presented with countless good opportunities? We shift from an earthly to an eternal perspective. We don't allow the lesser things (earthly concerns), to distract us from the better things (the concerns of the Lord).

How do we live well, making the most of our brief time on earth? We embrace eternity in the here and now. Charles Spurgeon once said, "Time is short. Eternity is long. It is only reasonable that this short life be lived in the light of eternity."

WHAT DOES IT MEAN?

Solomon, the teacher in Ecclesiastes, looks back on his life and shares with us what he's learned. The book is autobiographical, based on personal experience. Solomon offers insight into his successes and regrets while offering general observations about life. Ecclesiastes can feel disheartening for many, offering little hope for life under the sun. However, this wise teacher is trying to grab our attention. He desires listeners to grasp the reality of our mortality.

If life on earth is all there is, and it's lights out when we die, then everything we do, work, family, hobbies, or philanthropy, is meaningless. Nothing matters. Nothing we've accomplished, achieved, or acquired—the time we spent serving, working, and giving is worthless... unless we have a relationship with Jesus Christ.

The Hebrew word for meaningless is "hevel," relating to something without value.[1] Pursuing earthly goals, acquiring worth and possessions, and enjoying material advantages are not inherently wrong. It is when we become side-tracked by these earthly pursuits, allowing them to become our source of identity, worth, and joy, that we run into problems.

Therefore, in these opening lines, the teacher warns us about misplaced priorities and the inevitable consequences of a life focused too heavily on the earthly over the eternal. He urges us to stop pretending, leading us to abandon check-list Christianity; the "good enough" mentality so many of us embrace. Instead, we must surrender to following Christ in our motives, speech, and actions. We make the most of our time on earth by acknowledging God as Lord and submitting ourselves to His service and will. Each day, we must make a choice to prioritize the eternal over the temporary.

WHY DOES THIS MATTER?

So many of us are utterly exhausted because we have sacrificed ourselves on the altar of productivity, people-pleasing, personal success, and Pinterest-worthy lives. Christians have joined the rat race of the American Dream, believing that just because you can, you should. Why shouldn't you have that latest gadget? Why shouldn't you spend more money on making yourself look good and others jealous? You deserve it. You earned it. You are worth it. These are

---

[1] https://bibleproject.com/podcast/ecclesiastes

the mistruths whispered in our ears, enticing us to the insatiable pursuit of "more."

But what happens when you finally hit the magic number on the scale? Or you move to *the* neighborhood? That feeling of joy is fleeting. Once again, we find ourselves dissatisfied, disappointed, and disillusioned.

When we live with the eternal in mind, it informs how we live today. Living in light of eternity frees us from the burden of living an "important" life. There is liberation when we comprehend this is not our final destination. Those of us in Christ will experience eternity in the presence of our Creator. Accepting the gospel's wonderful gift allows us to live for God's glory alone, releasing the chains of worldly expectations, people pleasing, and proving our worth.

THE HARD HEART WORK

It's easy to *say* our faith is important, but do our lives *show* God is a priority? Glancing at our calendars and bank accounts will clearly indicate what we value.

Do you prioritize the eternal over the temporary?

Do you see any trends that suggest you might need to reconsider how you are spending your time and resources?

How does knowing that our lives are meaningless apart from Christ change where you invest your time and finances?

Life is short; invest in the things that have eternal significance.

PRAYER PROMPT

Heavenly Father, please help me to live with an eternal perspective. Help me to stay focused on You, choosing the things that bring You honor and glory. Help me fixate on the eternal. In Jesus' Name, Amen.

Day 2
WHAT IS THE POINT OF ALL OUR BUSYNESS?

READ: Ecclesiastes 1:5-11

The sun rises and the sun sets,
*   and hurries back to where it rises.*

⁶ The wind blows to the south
*   and turns to the north;*
*   round and round it goes,*
*   ever returning on its course.*

⁷ All streams flow into the sea,
*   yet the sea is never full.*
*   To the place the streams come from,*
*   there they return again.*

⁸ All things are wearisome,
*   more than one can say.*
*   The eye never has enough of seeing,*
*   nor the ear its fill of hearing.*

⁹ What has been will be again,
*   what has been done will be done again;*
*   there is nothing new under the sun.*

> **¹⁰** *Is there anything of which one can say,*
>   *"Look! This is something new"?*
>   *It was here already, long ago;*
>   *it was here before our time.*
>
> **¹¹** *No one remembers the former generations,*
>   *and even those yet to come*
>   *will not be remembered*
>   *by those who follow them.*

Every fall since high school, I have come down with what my parents affectionately termed "the Laura Flu." Traditionally, I am fever-free and have very few symptoms aside from utter exhaustion. My body will suddenly betray me, shut down, and yell, " I am done! Until you give me some rest, I am out!" It takes a full two to three days of sleeping for 16+ hours, complete isolation from the outside world, and avoidance of anything that requires brain power for me to fully recover.

As an achievement junkie, I tend to ignore the pleas my body naturally issues, warning me to slow down. I have convinced myself that the fate of the world rests on my shoulders. Who will sign up to take the cookies, lead the meeting, or create the perfect centerpiece for the party if I don't step up and step in? I genuinely fear everything might fall apart without my intervention.

Whenever I emerge from my cave and return to the real world after being knocked out by "the Laura Flu," I tell myself, "Next time, I am not going to let it get that bad; I am going to slow down!" And yet, a few weeks pass, and I find the persistent headache has come back, my stomach is once again in constant knots, and my sleep is

WHAT IS THE POINT OF ALL OUR BUSYNESS?

disturbed. This burning the candle at both ends, constant pushing and hustling, and break-neck pace always lead me to burn out.

I certainly can't be the lone victim of this vicious cycle. Might this sound familiar to you? Are you wired a bit like me? Why is it so hard for us to just slow down?

WHAT DOES IT MEAN?

In these opening verses, Solomon compares nature's organic rhythms to the frailty of human life. Solomon highlights the cyclical pattern of God's creation, which spans from the beginning of time and remains the same from generation to generation. Conversely, human life is brief. The next generation quickly forgets our impact.

Everyone is ultimately replaceable. Yet, we strive, hustle, and tirelessly attempt to make our mark, to be remembered, and have lasting significance. All of this leaves us burdened and weary. Mankind invests countless hours solidifying its place in history. While their names may be written in the history books, monuments resurrected in their honor, and holidays commemorate their greatness, only the Lord's name will endure the end of time (Exodus 3:15).

WHY DOES THIS MATTER?

Reading the above could feel like a wet blanket, but in reality, the words of Solomon are a breath of fresh air. We don't have to allow other people's opinions to persuade us to run the rat race of production, climb the corporate ladder, or let anything other than the pursuit of living life for the glory of God to consume us. We can lay down the need to prove ourselves, stop making decisions based on fear, and release the need to have and be it all.

Make the art, write the story, invent the application, and plan the event. The Lord has gifted you with unique talents, gifts, and abilities to serve Him. Use those skills to serve others, overflow from your cup as worship, and trade in performance for peace. When our identity is firmly rooted in Christ, we don't have to depend on what we do to define our worth. The title by our signature, marital status, or anything other than what God says about us has no lasting significance.

When we allow activity to become the end instead of the means, we invite chaos, stress, and discord into our lives and relationships. All of our "doing" is meaningless without Jesus at the center. This understanding gives us the freedom to prioritize what really matters. Let's focus our lives on what Scripture says has eternal value, and say no to what clutters our calendars, hearts, and minds.

THE HARD HEART WORK

Most of us could cut some things we see as essential, but are truly negotiable. Here are a few things in my life in which I felt the Holy Spirit speak to my heart.

Does your family need to be at the studio or sports complex five times a week, sacrificing connection around the table?

Do you need to serve on the nursery, greeter, hospitality, *and* special events committee, forgoing sleep so you can get it all done?

Is taking the job that pays more money worth the additional hours away and mental stress?

WHAT IS THE POINT OF ALL OUR BUSYNESS?

I encourage you to ask yourself the hard questions and challenge your motives for saying yes. Remember, while all of this can be good, we want to ask whether they are the best choice.

Stop trying so hard to leave a mark; choose peace over performance.

PRAYER PROMPT

Heavenly Father, I ask that you guide me as I seek to use my time, resources, and talents wisely. Help me remember that work centered around Your glory, and service to Your kingdom, are the only efforts with true eternal meaning. In Jesus' Name, Amen.

Day 3
THE SEARCH FOR MEANING

READ: Ecclesiastes 1:12-18

> ¹² I, the Teacher, was king over Israel in Jerusalem. ¹³ I applied my mind to study and to explore by wisdom all that is done under the heavens. What a heavy burden God has laid on mankind! ¹⁴ I have seen all the things that are done under the sun; all of them are meaningless, a chasing after the wind.
>
> ¹⁵ What is crooked cannot be straightened;
> what is lacking cannot be counted.
>
> ¹⁶ I said to myself, "Look, I have increased in wisdom more than anyone who has ruled over Jerusalem before me; I have experienced much of wisdom and knowledge." ¹⁷ Then I applied myself to the understanding of wisdom, and also of madness and folly, but I learned that this, too, is a chasing after the wind.
>
> ¹⁸ For with much wisdom comes much sorrow;
> the more knowledge, the more grief.

As the bread basket made its way around the table at a friend's wedding reception, my husband and I conversed with six total strangers. The opening lines went like this: "How do you know the couple? How long have you been married? Kids?" Next came the dreaded question: "What do you *do*?" Answering that last question made my heart race and my palms sweat. I felt sick. Yes, this may seem a bit dramatic, but it was no exaggeration for me.

Why did I feel it necessary to justify my current role as a full-time mother (ensuring I mentioned what I "did" before) to these people? Strangers, no less. This question was easily answered. My identity and self-esteem were primarily tied to my career. I was not trying to convince *them* that my current job as a stay-at-home mom was important. No, it was another attempt to convince myself.

You see, for years, the title after my signature (*not* the inscription God penned by name) defined me and validated my self-worth. It has taken years to step away from this self-sufficiency and self-imposed identity. If I am being honest, I still struggle with the fact that my identity is not in what I do but in Who I belong to.

WHAT DOES IT MEAN?

Solomon was a man who had it all, yet at the end of his life, he reflected on how nothing wholly satisfied him. The more he had, the more he wanted, sound familiar? Acquiring more wives, houses, and land sometimes provided temporary contentment, but the end result was emptiness. Solomon had the gift of wisdom and discernment, but he kept allowing himself to be distracted by worldly success and significance. Scripture describes Solomon as the wisest man that ever lived (1 Kings 3:12), and when he acted out of godly insight, Solomon achieved great things. However, Solomon's knowledge was often a stumbling block, as he chose to ignore God's ways and depend on his own judgment and intellect.

In these last verses of chapter one, Solomon speaks as someone who walked the path of self-indulgence, self-promotion, and self-assurance only to discover that relying on his own capabilities was burdensome. He became preoccupied with exalting his name in the kingdom rather than bringing God glory.

Pursuing wisdom, growing a career, and achieving a goal for personal gain will only lead to an empty existence. Solomon believed increased knowledge and a bolstered resume would lead to success and happiness. But, he concludes that When hope is placed in what we can achieve, there is no guarantee of joy, peace, or prosperity.

WHY DOES IT MATTER?

Millions of dollars are spent each year on self-help, living a great life now, and learning how to make this your best year. We are consumed with the idea that if we just had a better job, a smaller waist size, joined a new group of friends, took more vacations, or spent more time with our spouse, *then* we would finally be happy. *Then*... that ache in our souls would go away. Like addicts, we fill the void in our lives, convincing ourselves that the next "hit" will be the answer to our problems. It's the definition of insanity: repeating the same actions and expecting a different outcome.

We believe the age-old lie that the serpent whispered to Eve, "God is holding out on you" (Genesis 3:5). Solomon, just like Eve, discovered that gaining more wisdom and taking on more than what God intended for your life, doesn't lead to freedom. It leads to captivity. We become slaves to the quest for more. More running ourselves ragged to achieve what only God can—our salvation from a meaningless life.

THE SEARCH FOR MEANING

Scripture tells us that by grace, we have been saved through faith. It is a gift from the Lord (Ephesians 2:8-9). Salvation is through Christ alone. It is not Jesus and our good works. It is not Jesus and our service. It is not Jesus and our Christian checklist. It is simply Jesus.

THE HARD HEART WORK

Tim Keller defines an idol as " anything that absorbs your heart and imagination more than God, anything you seek to give you what only God can give."

What idols are present in your life?

What controls your happiness, your peace, or your worth? What in your life, if absent, would cause your world to fall apart?

What step can you take to start surrendering these idols to the Lord?

Your identity is not in what you do but in who are in Christ.

PRAYER PROMPT

Heavenly Father, I am so easily distracted by promises of a world that never delivers. You created me out of love and desire for my good and Your glory. Help me to stay focused on you, choosing biblical wisdom over our own. Help me remember that my identity is secure in Your work on the cross. In Jesus' Name, Amen.

Day 4
TAKE THE VACATION BUT MONDAY IS COMING

READ: Ecclesiastes 2:1-11

> ¹ I said to myself, "Come now, I will test you with pleasure to find out what is good." But that also proved to be meaningless. ² "Laughter," I said, "is madness. And what does pleasure accomplish?" ³ I tried cheering myself with wine, and embracing folly—my mind still guiding me with wisdom. I wanted to see what was good for people to do under the heavens during the few days of their lives.
>
> ⁴ I undertook great projects: I built houses for myself and planted vineyards. ⁵ I made gardens and parks and planted all kinds of fruit trees in them. ⁶ I made reservoirs to water groves of flourishing trees. ⁷ I bought male and female slaves and had other slaves who were born in my house. I also owned more herds and flocks than anyone in Jerusalem before me. ⁸ I amassed silver and gold for myself, and the treasure of kings and provinces. I acquired male and female singers, and a harem as well—the delights of a man's heart. ⁹ I became greater by far than anyone in Jerusalem before me. In all this my wisdom stayed with me.

TAKE THE VACATION BUT MONDAY IS COMING

> [10] *I denied myself nothing my eyes desired;*
> *I refused my heart no pleasure.*
> *My heart took delight in all my labor,*
> *and this was the reward for all my toil.*
>
> [11] *Yet when I surveyed all that my hands had done*
> *and what I had toiled to achieve,*
> *everything was meaningless, a chasing after the wind;*
> *nothing was gained under the sun.*

As I fiddled with the coffee maker, reluctantly programming the automatic brew for 6:00 a.m., I muttered, " I need a vacation from my vacation."

It never fails, when I return home from a planned trip, I always experience the "vacation letdown." After a week of slow mornings, rich food, and late nights, I struggle to get back into the groove of life. But what's funny is that by the third or fourth day of vacation, I become annoyed with the lack of schedule, my stomach hurts from the decadent food and lack of consistent exercise, and I tout, " I am ready to get back to reality."

While on vacation, I make mental checklists of chores, errands, and issues that needed attention as I longed to return to "normal life." Yet, before our car pulled into the driveway, I was planning our next getaway. What a paradox. We complain about our work, but when allowed to rest and relax, we struggle to be present and enjoy the moment. Humans are fickle; rarely content with our current circumstances because we place too high an importance on finding lasting gratification in our work and play.

Embracing Eternity IN THE HERE AND NOW

WHAT DOES IT MEAN?

Pleasure, leisure, cutting up, letting loose, and having a good time aren't necessarily bad. The ability to relax, share a meal with friends, and find enjoyment in a hobby are good gifts from a gracious God. Conversely, taking pride in your job, celebrating your successes, and working towards a goal are blessings from the Lord. Solomon shares in these few verses that experiencing pleasure or finding joy in our work is not the problem. It is a problem when we seek complete satisfaction, that sense of euphoria, from earthly entertainment and benchmarks of success. We step aside from God's plan for His children.

In verses 3-10, Solomon goes into depth about how he attempted to rely on human gratification to provide him a sense of meaning and fill the void in his life only a genuine relationship with God could supply. Solomon was one of the wealthiest men in the Bible. He had everything he wanted. He was the person everyone wanted to be. He threw lavish parties with wine that flowed freely and continuously replenished food. Solomon built numerous vineyards, houses, and parks to quiet his mind and still his spirit. He grew his labor force, increased his livestock, acquired riches from other kings, and even purchased his own choir. This famous ruler had over 700 wives and 300 concubines. He denied himself nothing.

Solomon's goal was to be greater than anyone in Jerusalem—and he was. Yet, he was also one of the most unfulfilled. Solomon looked back on all his attempts to secure enduring happiness and remarked that none had any lasting consequence. For all his toil, grand palaces, abundance of women, and immense wealth, in the end, none of it ever satisfied.

TAKE THE VACATION BUT MONDAY IS COMING

WHY DOES IT MATTER?

Slogans such as "You work hard, so you should play hard, too!" entice and justify us.

These marketing campaigns show the family having a blast on their Caribbean cruise, but they don't show the maxed-out credit cards and arguments over money resulting from overspending. The sports team shouts, "Your kids are missing out!" when you don't sign-up for the team that will monopolize every weekend this summer. Still, they neglect to share about the physical, mental, and spiritual stress of living life at a break-neck speed and forgoing biblical community on Sundays. The TV or social media ads declare, "You've labored your whole life; you deserve the luxury car..." sold by a dealership that is more than happy to let you sign and drive as they quickly glance over the fiscal burden of such a purchase. But when that new car smell wears off, so does the thrill, yet you're stuck in your contract.

Owning possessions, enjoying life, and spending money are not the problem. The issue is that we humans do good things wrong. Too many people bandage their pain with a shiny new object instead of dealing with the hurt, coping with the grief, and accepting the reality of life. But the shine of self-pacification always fades, leaving us on a quest for the latest and improved to take its place. It is a vicious cycle; the endless pursuit of joy trapped in false promises. God was here at the outset. He is the Alpha and Omega, the beginning and the end. While there are other things in our lives worth investing in, our marriages, families, church, a relationship with the Lord should be our highest priority.

THE HARD HEART WORK

Friend, do not be dismayed if you recognize unworthy substitutions you've allowed to be your source of happiness. That's God's love, shedding light and understanding on areas of our hearts and lives where He offers a better way.

As you read through today's devotional, did the Lord expose an area you have allowed to be your source of fulfillment?

Are there areas that the Holy Spirit is prompting you to examine? The amount of time, money, or heart space you have allocated towards pleasure or profession?

Do you spend more time on self-gratification than serving others? Are your weeks and weekends so full that church has become an option?

We can enjoy our professions and pastimes, but lasting fulfillment comes from the Lord.

LET'S PRAY

Heavenly Father, thank you for the blessing of enjoying both times of labor and rest. I am grateful for the opportunity to break from our work, soak in your creation, spend time with family, and rejuvenate and restore our bodies. Help me to keep the proper perspective and be cautious of celebrating the created, not the Creator. In Jesus' name, Amen.

Day 5
NOT ALL THINGS ARE WORTH KNOWING

READ: Ecclesiastes 2:12-16

> [12] Then I turned my thoughts to consider wisdom,
> and also madness and folly.
> What more can the king's successor do
> than what has already been done?
>
> [13] I saw that wisdom is better than folly,
> just as light is better than darkness.
>
> [14] The wise have eyes in their heads,
> while the fool walks in the darkness;
> but I came to realize
> that the same fate overtakes them both.
>
> [15] Then I said to myself,
> "The fate of the fool will overtake me also.
> What then do I gain by being wise?"
> I said to myself,
> "This too is meaningless."
>
> [16] For the wise, like the fool, will not be long remembered;
> the days have already come when both have been forgotten.
> Like the fool, the wise too must die!

I love to read. Give me a dreary winter's day, a chunky cable-knit blanket, a bottomless cup of coffee, and I could sit for hours snuggled on the couch, nose in a book. I'll never forget when my senior year English teacher shared with the class why she enjoyed reading. "It makes you smarter," she quipped. As someone who understood they weren't naturally the most intelligent person in the room but was often the most driven, I decided then and there that I would become a reader.

When I wanted to learn how to make lasting impressions, I purchased "How to Win Friends and Influence People." When I tried cooking French cuisine, I snagged a copy of Julia Child's "Mastering the Art of French Cooking." When I decided to get serious about my faith, I checked out a copy of "Knowing God" by J.I. Packer.

Learning a new skill, expanding your capabilities, and pursuing a deeper understanding of the Bible are all good as long as they don't lead us down the path of self-reliance. Knowledge is the driving force behind helping or hindering, promoting or preventing and deepening and dividing. Knowledge is the acquisition of information; wisdom is the ability to discern how to use that information wisely. Many people possess knowledge, but few know how to live wisely.

WHAT DOES IT MEAN?

When King David, Solomon's father, passed away, he left Solomon to oversee the kingdom. Understandably nervous about taking on such an influential role, Solomon was uncertain about his ability to rule well. The Lord spoke to Solomon in a dream and told Solomon that he could ask for anything (1 Kings 3:5). Solomon responded, "So give your servant a discerning heart to govern your people and distinguish between right and wrong. Who can govern these great people of yours?" (1 Kings 3:9). The Lord granted Solomon this desire. Even greater, God declared there would never be anyone as knowledgeable as Solomon. He would be known as the wisest man in history!

Solomon heard directly from the Lord that he would always be the most intelligent man in the room. Yet, he spent much of his life trying to gain increased knowledge, decipher the mysteries of life, and solve every problem. The unquenchable desire for omniscience left Solomon exhausted. Ultimately, Solomon concluded that it didn't matter how much you knew because the wise and the foolish suffer the same fate: death.

WHY DOES IT MATTER?

We put a lot of stock in measuring intelligence. Parents boast about their baby's first words, elementary school kids work diligently on special projects to display for parents, seniors anxiously await their standardized test scores, and college graduates proudly include their GPA on their resumes. However, my husband and I like to remind our girls, someone will always be more competent in the room. It is wise not to let a test score, a gold star, or the title next to your signature go to your head.

While increased understanding can be helpful, not all knowledge is beneficial. I think about the teenagers at my church. Thanks to 30-second videos on the internet, they can share with me how to make your manicure last longer, the key to a perfectly baked pie, and what someone in China ate for dinner last night. Their brains are indeed filled with a lot of information, but I am not convinced all the content consumed allows them to gain wisdom.

Before you assume I am a social media downer (unless it's doom scrolling, that's not helping anyone's mental state), I am not. I've enjoyed multiple laughs and snagged helpful hints from these tiny squares. At a time in history when information consumption is at an all-time high, we must examine the content we consume. Scripture tells us that spiritual transformation happens when we renew our minds. Filtering our intake through the lens of eternity by filling our minds with timeless truth instead of temporary tips brings true transformation.

THE HARD HEART WORK

The old saying goes, "You are who your friends are." This is true of our media diet. What you put in is what will come out. Take a second look at your bookshelf, or open the phone usage app, and see what consumes most of your attention.

Are your shelves filled with novels you've stayed up late devouring while your Bible is clothed in dust?

Does your search history speak of your unquenchable need to know every detail about the Royal Family, yet the Bible App on your phone goes unopened?

Can you sing every lyric of your favorite songs, but committing Scripture to memory seems impossible?

Acquiring knowledge doesn't guarantee that life will be lived wisely.

NOT ALL THINGS ARE WORTH KNOWING

LET'S PRAY

Heavenly Father, thank you for giving me Your Word. May I never take for granted the ability to read Scripture. Help me to hide Your Word in my heart, commit the verses to memory, and meditate on its truth day and night. Grant me the wisdom and discernment that only comes from You. In Jesus' Name, Amen.

Day 6
WORK TO LIVE, NOT LIVE TO WORK

READ: Ecclesiastes 2:17-26

> ¹⁷ So I hated life, because the work that is done under the sun was grievous to me. All of it is meaningless, a chasing after the wind. ¹⁸ I hated all the things I had toiled for under the sun, because I must leave them to the one who comes after me. ¹⁹ And who knows whether that person will be wise or foolish? Yet they will have control over all the fruit of my toil into which I have poured my effort and skill under the sun. This too is meaningless. ²⁰ So my heart began to despair over all my toilsome labor under the sun. ²¹ For a person may labor with wisdom, knowledge and skill, and then they must leave all they own to another who has not toiled for it. This too is meaningless and a great misfortune. ²² What do people get for all the toil and anxious striving with which they labor under the sun? ²³ All their days their work is grief and pain; even at night their minds do not rest. This too is meaningless.
>
> ²⁴ A person can do nothing better than to eat and drink and find satisfaction in their own toil. This too, I see, is from the hand of God, ²⁵ for without him, who can eat or find enjoyment? ²⁶ To the person who pleases him, God gives wisdom, knowledge and happiness, but to the sinner he gives the task of gathering

WORK TO LIVE, NOT LIVE TO WORK

and storing up wealth to hand it over to the one who pleases God. This too is meaningless, a chasing after the wind.

"Wait, she is going to take over all my clients?"

I'd recently been promoted to a new role within the organization. Before moving to my new position, my boss asked if I would transition my clients to the woman who would be taking over my job. She'd only worked with the company for a few months. I had spent years developing this list of contacts.

I moved to the area and started from scratch. I slept on my brother's couch for six months and worked out of my car for almost a year before my company invested in an actual office. While on maternity leave, I still checked in with my clients to ensure they were cared for. I dealt with issues on Christmas Eve, took calls on vacation, and woke up before the sun rose to balance motherhood and career. Some of these clients were guests at my wedding. We exchanged Christmas cards. They were family to me. I'd sacrificed so much for this job, and for what, for someone else to just take it over?

In most cases, no one will value your work as much as you because you had to give up something in exchange for success. And that's where we find Solomon in these following verses—reminding us to hold our work loosely because, at some point, it will go to someone else. And when it does, it may all fall apart.

WHAT DOES IT MEAN?

These verses seek to answer the question, "What does man gain for all his hard work?" The response is: "Not a whole lot." Work is a blessing from God. He gave Adam and Eve work in the garden, so we know that labor itself is not bad. But, like many other areas of our lives, we've turned careers into idols. Nothing we produce lasts forever. No matter how valiant our efforts, we will always be unable to leave a permanent mark on the world. Yet, we sacrifice much of our lives climbing the ladder of success, proving our worth, and making a name for ourselves.

To further illustrate the futility of our work, Solomon shares his frustration that everything he labored and sacrificed for, will ultimately go to someone else. His successors will have full access to his achievements and reap the benefits of success without having invested time or effort. Solomon becomes deeply grieved as he thinks about his life's work being handed over to someone else, only to be squandered—and in Solomon's case, that's precisely what happened. Solomon ruled in Israel for 40 years, leaving his kingdom to his son, Rehoboam. The kingdom was split into two territories shortly after Rehoboam came into power. Most of the land, along with the political power, went to Jeroboam, Solomon's previous advisor, who openly criticized the wise king's leadership.

However, the succession of wealth is a part of life. We work tirelessly at a skill, study for years to master a craft, or dedicate decades to becoming the best in our field. But, in the end, it all goes to someone else, and our mark on the earth is like a footprint in the sand. The imprint only briefly remains and then is quickly washed away.

WHY DOES THIS MATTER?

In the fictional novel, *The Invisible Life of Addie LaRue*, another author challenges readers to contemplate the consequences of

WORK TO LIVE, NOT LIVE TO WORK

immortality. In the story, the main character, Addie LaRue, strikes a deal to live an "invisible life" in exchange for her escape from an unwanted marriage. Her wish was granted. She was freed from permanent connection to a spouse. However, this freedom came at a hefty price. Addie forfeited her full identity. For the rest of her days, she would exist but not be recognized or remembered. She would be unable to leave any lasting impression, permanent mark, or legacy. While there are definite drawbacks to this reality, I wonder how differently we might live if we knew nothing we did, not even our individual identities, would be remembered.

We've all heard the stories of people who seek forgiveness from their families and friends at the end of their lives for spending more time working than with them. It seems the regret of misplaced priorities doesn't discriminate. From the CEO to the PTO, we place a high value on our careers as a society. And to what end? For some extra padding in our bank accounts, a couple more square feet, a few more trips to the beach? Was sacrificing our relationships, physical health, and spiritual formation worth it? Most would answer with a resounding "no."

God created work; it is part of our human existence. Solomon is not implying that we abandon our jobs. His words aren't meant to criticize a successful career or incite shame for having responsibilities outside our families, friendships, and faith. Instead, he is encouraging us to live with the proper perspective. We were made to work to live, not live to work.

May our efforts reflect that the only name remembered through eternity is the Lord's.

Embracing Eternity IN THE HERE AND NOW

THE HARD HEART WORK

There's a reason Solomon doesn't give a one-size-fits-all recommendation for work-life balance. What's beneficial for one person may not function well for another. It is not the amount of time spent advancing our careers, toiling away, or laboring years of life that matters, but the heart's motivation.

Are you working for a promotion because you believe that once gained, you will finally feel valued?

Have you allowed work to crash vacations, family time, or special events because your job makes you feel important?

Take some time to examine the role of work in your life. Are you using the Lord's gifts and talents to bring Him glory or yourself? Or have you allowed your job to become your identity, security blanket, or financial comfort?

Our work won't be remembered, so don't sacrifice relationships for productivity.

PRAYER PROMPT

Heavenly Father, I am grateful for the opportunity to labor for the kingdom. Help me keep the proper perspective, using our talents to glorify You, not ourselves. Let me enjoy the benefits of hard work and a restorative sabbath. In Jesus' Name, Amen.

Day 7
NOTHING LASTS FOREVER

READ: Ecclesiastes 3:1-8

*³:¹ There is a time for everything,
and a season for every activity under the heavens:*

*² a time to be born and a time to die,
a time to plant and a time to uproot,*

*³ a time to kill and a time to heal,
a time to tear down and a time to build,*

*⁴ a time to weep and a time to laugh,
a time to mourn and a time to dance,*

*⁵ a time to scatter stones and a time to gather them,
a time to embrace and a time to refrain from embracing,*

*⁶ a time to search and a time to give up,
a time to keep and a time to throw away,*

*⁷ a time to tear and a time to mend,
a time to be silent and a time to speak,*

*⁸ a time to love and a time to hate,
a time for war and a time for peace.*

Embracing Eternity IN THE HERE AND NOW

I thought about returning to school when my girls were in the "baby to preschool" era. A part of me knew it wasn't the best time, but people go to school, have jobs, and raise families all the time. Surely I could do it, too!

However, I neglected to consider this span of sleepless nights, my husband's job change, and the obligations I'd committed to. While my husband didn't discourage me from moving forward with the classes, he did encourage me to consider how this extra commitment would fit into an already packed calendar. Thankfully, I listened to his advice and other Christian influences and decided this really "wasn't the right season."

If you're like me, we often think we are making the most of our time by maxing out our calendars, choosing to "sleep when we are dead," and forgoing margin in our days. We proceed with our plans even when it's not the right moment. Just as seasons change, so will the periods of our lives—each ordained by God. Nothing is by chance.

WHAT DOES IT MEAN?

Ecclesiastes 3:1-8 is one of the most quoted Scripture passages by Christians and non-believers alike. In this passage, Solomon affirms that God is not only the author of life, the supreme judge, sovereign ruler, and ultimate authority; He also appoints seasons.

In poetic form, Solomon contrasts fourteen different life experiences or seasons. Each pairing (apart from the first comparison in verse 2) describes the relationship between human actions and the ultimate result of their labor. The Lord created the world with a specific design. Just as the seasons exist for a particular purpose in nature, so do the intervals of our lives. Life moves from one situation to the next, whether or not we are prepared for changing circumstances.

WHY DOES IT MATTER?

Have you ever felt that there are times when life seems to fly by, and others seem to drag on? Time is consistent. The hours and minutes are always moving at the same pace, but depending on what is going on in our lives, it impacts us differently. Solomon's observation about seasons "under the sun" is meant as a reminder of the brevity and futility of life. Even if our lives are considered long by human standards, our time on earth is a vapor, a mist, a blink. Our existence will be here and then gone.

Unlike previous verses, Solomon shares the various activities done under the heavens but doesn't remark if they are good or bad. Which are wise? Which are foolish? He does not say. These verses are descriptive, not prescriptive, meaning Solomon is making an observation, not giving us a list of rules on how we should live. By combining these contrasting seasons, Solomon reminds us that neither good nor bad will last forever.

If your present circumstances are dire, know this suffering won't last forever. And while your prayers may not be answered entirely on this side of eternity, one day, those of us in Christ will experience life without the presence of sin. Hallelujah!

Conversely, if you are in a season of celebration, lift up gratitude to the Lord for His blessings! Life is cyclic. Our days are repetitive. We experience years and decades of monotony and routine. Seeking meaning in our work, relationships, bank accounts, followers, or other earthly pursuits will only frustrate us. Instead of investing in the here today gone tomorrow, let's put our hope in the eternal—a relationship with Jesus. The Lord will never abandon His children.

THE HARD HEART WORK

Ecclesiastes 3 reminds us that God appointed the seasons. Nothing about you, where you live, your family, or your current circumstances—are by chance. Think about your current context. Does it bring you comfort or concern that no era lasts forever?

If you are in a season of suffering, how can you praise God even when your heart is heavy?

If you find yourself overwhelmed or exhausted, take time today to write down your responsibilities and see if there is anything you can lay down this season.

If you experience joy and contentment, prioritize offering gratitude to the Lord daily and look for ways to help those who are burdened and struggling.

Remember that whatever season you are in, God is sovereign over it all. Keep trusting in God's purpose and plan.

PRAYER PROMPT

Heavenly Father, thank you for the gift of life. I know you are the author of time, and nothing is outside your control. Teach me to number my days and remember You and Your faithfulness in every season. In Jesus' Name, Amen.

Day 8
KEEPING OUR BAGS PACKED

READ: Ecclesiastes 3:9-15

> *⁹ What do workers gain from their toil? ¹⁰ I have seen the burden God has laid on the human race. ¹¹ He has made everything beautiful in its time. He has also set eternity in the human heart; yet no one can fathom what God has done from beginning to end. ¹² I know that there is nothing better for people than to be happy and to do good while they live. ¹³ That each of them may eat and drink, and find satisfaction in all their toil—this is the gift of God. ¹⁴ I know that everything God does will endure forever; nothing can be added to it and nothing taken from it. God does it so that people will fear him.*
>
> *¹⁵ Whatever is has already been,*
> *and what will be has been before;*
> *and God will call the past to account.*

It bothers my husband that I never unpack my suitcase when traveling, no matter the length of our trip. Sure, I may hang out my dresses and take out my toiletries, but for the most part, I live out of my bag. Conversely, he unloads his suitcase, arranging his shoes neatly in the closet. When asked one time why I "refuse" to unpack,

Embracing Eternity IN THE HERE AND NOW

I simply said, "Because we will only be here for a while, then we are going home."

If only I were more committed to remembering that this world is not my final destination, home, or only place. Too often, I let temporary things distract me from the eternal. My decisions, reactions, and actions reflect someone living for this world, not for eternity.

God created us for eternity. We are strangers in a foreign land, visitors waiting to go to our eternal home. We feel restlessness and unease, and no matter how excellent the accommodations are, we aren't meant to unpack our lives in the here and now fully. Our destiny is heaven. Our place is with our Creator.

WHAT DOES THIS MEAN?

As we've covered already, Ecclesiastes highlights the pitfalls of life in a fallen world. Solomon draws our attention to these temporal failings in an attempt to drive us into the arms of our Savior—Jesus. Man's chief purpose is to know God and make Him known. Therefore, it was never God's desire for us to chase the momentary substitutes of this world. Earthly pursuits weren't designed to give us lasting contentment. We cannot satisfy the craving to be known through human creations; only our Creator can fulfill these desires of our hearts.

Solomon remarks that the "Lord has made everything beautiful in His time," emphasizing *His* time. What little control humans may think we have over our lives results from a gracious, merciful God who allows us to act within His sovereign will. When we understand that our time in this world is only temporary, we stop chasing after what the world says will make us happy and enjoy life's simple pleasures given to us by a loving Father.

Knowing that our days are numbered, how then should we live our lives?

WHY DOES IT MATTER?

Our verses today are some of my favorites in Scripture. I find such comfort in knowing that the ache I feel, the sense that I am never really quite at home, is my earthly body longing to be in the presence of the Lord. I can stop trying so hard to prove myself, be validated by others, and say yes just because everyone else is doing it. Because, ultimately, my only fulfillment is found in and through Him.

Solomon asserts that this constant pushing, hustling for more, and the continual need to prove only leads to exhaustion and burnout. And for what purpose? To leave a mark? We are eternal beings, so when we try to fill our lives with temporary things, it will always leave us longing for more. We must maintain proper perspective while there is breath in our lungs to enjoy the gift of life and the Lord's blessings. But always remember, you weren't made for the here and now. You were created for eternity!

THE HARD HEART WORK

Friend, I hope you read the above-mentioned words and felt a weight lifted from your shoulders. How does knowing that you were created for eternity change where you spend your time, energy, and resources?

Embracing Eternity IN THE HERE AND NOW

Think about your spiritual bags. Are they packed and ready to meet your Maker, or have you settled into your earthly digs?

Take some time and really think through your life. Where do you invest your time, resources, and energy? What do you place a high value on? Would you say your priorities look more like the current culture or a life that points to Christ?

You were created for eternity; make sure you aren't living like this world is your permanent home.

PRAYER PROMPT

Heavenly Father, please help me remember that I was made for eternity. The eternal glory that awaits us pales in comparison to what this world offers. Let me lean into the Holy Spirit to live with proper reverence, worship, and fear of You. In Jesus' Name, Amen.

Day 9
LIFE ISN'T FAIR

READ: Ecclesiastes 3:16-22

> ¹⁶ And I saw something else under the sun:
> In the place of judgment—wickedness was there,
> in the place of justice—wickedness was there.
>
> ¹⁷ I said to myself,
> "God will bring into judgment
> both the righteous and the wicked,
> for there will be a time for every activity,
> a time to judge every deed."
>
> ¹⁸ I also said to myself, "As for humans, God tests them so that they may see that they are like the animals. ¹⁹ Surely the fate of human beings is like that of the animals; the same fate awaits them both: As one dies, so dies the other. All have the same breath; humans have no advantage over animals. Everything is meaningless. ²⁰ All go to the same place; all come from dust, and to dust all return. ²¹ Who knows if the human spirit rises upward and if the spirit of the animal goes down into the earth?"

Embracing Eternity IN THE HERE AND NOW

> *²² So I saw that there is nothing better for a person than to enjoy their work, because that is their lot. For who can bring them to see what will happen after them?*

In an authentic and raw moment, my friend shared with our accountability group her current wrestling with God with. "I am struggling to see God at work in this situation; I know life isn't always fair, but it feels like God is letting evil win!" As soon as the words left her lips, she apologized for her full transparency and stressed that she was frustrated, but her faith was fully intact.

"You don't need to apologize; I get it," affirmed one woman.

"Yes, I've been there. I know exactly what you are going through," another friend offered.

"I am just thankful that someone else feels that way sometimes, too. I worry that I am a bad Christian because I question God when I can't see Him at work," I openly admitted.

My friend's embarrassment quickly subsided. The confessions from the other ladies in our group comforted her. She wasn't alone in her struggle. Here was a group of godly women, whose faith was grounded in Scripture, yet battled moments of doubt and uncertainty. Having faith doesn't remove the hardships around us. But, it does help us realize that no matter what God has planned for His people, He can be trusted, even when we don't understand His ways.

LIFE ISN'T FAIR

WHAT DOES IT MEAN?

These last verses in chapter 3 conclude Solomon's observations about the seasons. He closes this section with a sobering reminder that there is also a time for judgment. This is not the last time Solomon will speak about God's judgment, as it is one of the central themes in the book of Ecclesiastes. [2]

Solomon asks the same questions most of us are asking today: " Why is there so much injustice in the world?" Why do the wicked seem to prosper and the righteous seem to struggle? However, this worldly king quickly turns his attention from questioning the existence of injustice to acknowledging God as the ultimate justice. He will judge the righteous and the unrighteous at the proper time.

WHY DOES IT MATTER?

British philosopher, John Stuart Mill, also comments on the apparent success of those with questionable motives. "Bad men need nothing more to compass their ends, than that good men should look on and do nothing." Sometimes, it feels that God is more concerned with policing His children than punishing the wicked and those who openly rebel against Him. God's "inaction" can suggest to us that He allows corrupt nations, morally bankrupt leaders, and wicked, vile people to continue to succeed in their plans.

Countless times, I've held my hands up to the Lord (even shook my fists a time or two), frustrated at His permitting evil to go

---

[2] MacArthur, J. (2013). *MacArthur Study Bible: New International Version*. Thomas Nelson.

"unchecked" in the world. I struggle to see His goodness and question His love, compassion, mercy, and grace. Yet, God is not surprised or offended by His children's lack of understanding. He reminds us in Scripture that " His ways are not our ways" (Isaiah 55:8) and "no one can comprehend His thoughts" (1 Corinthians 2:11).

While our wrestling doesn't shock our Heavenly Father, He desires that we continue to trust in Him even when we can't understand. How do we do this? We go back to Scripture, renewing our minds and reminding ourselves of the countless times the Lord has faithfully kept His promises. We cling to these truths as we accept, "In due season God will judge everyone, both good and bad, for all their deeds" (Ecclesiastes 3:17).

THE HARD HEART WORK

Think about a time when you've found yourself wrestling with God. It's easy to question God when we don't have the luxury of "peeking behind the heavenly curtain."

Do you think there's a way to "wrestle-well" with the Lord? How can you learn to accept a situation when you want to argue with God?

If you are doubting, wondering why, or frustrated with the Lord, how can you remind yourself of God's character and His promises?

2 Peter 3:9 says, "The Lord is not slow in keeping his promise, as some understand slowness. Instead, He is patient with you, not wanting anyone to perish, but everyone to come to repentance." How does understanding God's patience in leading us as sinners to repentance change your perspective on what feels like Him allowing evil to prevail?

LIFE ISN'T FAIR

God is still working all things for our good and His glory, even when we don't understand or agree with his actions or inaction in the world.

LET'S PRAY

Heavenly Father, forgive me when I doubt, question, and criticize You. I have limited understanding and can't begin to comprehend how You are working and moving in the world. Please grant me comfort and assurance that you will one day bring every deed into judgment. In Jesus' Name, Amen.

Day 10
PEOPLE NEED PEOPLE

READ: Ecclesiastes 4:1-12

> ¹ Again I looked and saw all the oppression that was taking place under the sun:
> I saw the tears of the oppressed—
> and they have no comforter;
> power was on the side of their oppressors—
> and they have no comforter.
>
> ² And I declared that the dead,
> who had already died,
> are happier than the living,
> who are still alive.
>
> ³ But better than both
> is the one who has never been born,
> who has not seen the evil
> that is done under the sun.
>
> ⁴ And I saw that all toil and all achievement spring from one person's envy of another. This too is meaningless, a chasing after the wind.
>
> ⁵ Fools fold their hands
> and ruin themselves.

PEOPLE NEED PEOPLE

⁶ Better one handful with tranquility
than two handfuls with toil
and chasing after the wind.

⁷ Again I saw something meaningless under the sun:

⁸ There was a man all alone;
he had neither son nor brother.
There was no end to his toil,
yet his eyes were not content with his wealth.
"For whom am I toiling," he asked,
"and why am I depriving myself of enjoyment?"
This too is meaningless—
a miserable business!

⁹ Two are better than one,
because they have a good return for their labor:

¹⁰ If either of them falls down,
one can help the other up.
But pity anyone who falls
and has no one to help them up.

¹¹ Also, if two lie down together, they will keep warm.
But how can one keep warm alone?

¹² Though one may be overpowered,
two can defend themselves.
A cord of three strands is not quickly broken.

It's not hard to remember the days, weeks, months (and in some places, a year or more) of regulations around gathering, or should I say, the lack of gathering. Once we all seemed to emerge on the other side of 2020, community life was re-established, little by little, and I was asked to speak at our annual ladies' luncheon.

Embracing Eternity IN THE HERE AND NOW

Prior to this, I'd never experienced a time when I couldn't gather in the community, so I was overjoyed to spend time fellowshipping with my sisters in Christ once again. I shared how wonderful it was to be fellowshipping with one another. I hadn't realized how I had taken the gift of gathering for granted. In the richness of that moment, I thanked the Lord for the opportunity to come together.

We crave connection. Christians need to be part of a local church community—a real-life, in-person meeting, not just a digital encounter. There really is no substitute for human interaction. Human connection isn't just a desire; it's an intrinsic need. We were created for it!

WHAT DOES IT MEAN?

As we study the following chapters, Solomon will address how we can quickly become frustrated or disappointed in our relationships, especially when our expectations of others are unmet. The first few verses of chapter four address the ramifications of political abuse of power when those who are meant to protect instead oppress and inflict harm on others.

Solomon observes how easy it is to compare ourselves with others in all areas of our lives, particularly in our work. We set ourselves up for failure when our success is measured by how well we outperform someone else. It's a miserable existence trying to constantly one-up someone else, surpass, or outdo others. It is a recipe for bitterness, discontentment, disappointment, and above all relational isolation.

In this last section, Solomon emphasizes the importance of relationships. The fruits of our labor are better enjoyed with someone, and life is better with people to share it with. He illustrates that man is better off with a partner—"two are better than one"—and lists numerous practical reasons for living in a community.

WHY DOES IT MATTER?

Relationships are tricky, Amen?!

I get it; it is hard to love the people that drive you crazy. But, we are called to community. Life is better together, not just for having an extra pair of hands to help wrangle the kids or hang the picture, but to experience the God-ordained connection between humans. We need more real-time over Facetime, a show of emotion over emoji-filled texts, and conversations in homes over skimming through highlight reels. People need people, mess and all. Authentic relationships are beautiful!

Often, as a result of spending time in community, we can be tempted to judge others or fall into the comparison trap. God has created everyone with the same purpose, to glorify Him, but with different skills, talents, and assignments. Cheer on your sister in Christ, partner with her, and remember, her gain is not your loss.

THE HARD HEART WORK

Family, church, friends, work, all types of "family" are messy! Knowing that we are called to community, what steps can you take to "love the ones who drive us crazy?"

Is there a person that sparks a battle of comparison in you? How does thinking of her as a partner instead of competition change how you see yourself and that relationship?

Hurt experienced from church is difficult to overcome, yet Scripture commands, not suggests, that we "not neglect gathering with the saints." If this has been your experience, how can you let go of the chains of resentment and experience the freedom found in forgiveness?

We were created for and crave community. Relationships are messy but worth it!

LET'S PRAY

Heavenly Father, I am grateful that you saw it wasn't good for man to be alone and gave us the gift of community. Please help me in my relationships to love openly and forgive quickly. Guide me and direct my conversations and interactions with others. In Jesus' Name, Amen.

Day 11
THE DANGERS OF A CHECKLIST CHRISTIANITY

READ: Ecclesiastes 4:13-16 & 5:1-7

> ¹³ *Better a poor but wise youth than an old but foolish king who no longer knows how to heed a warning.* ¹⁴ *The youth may have come from prison to the kingship, or he may have been born in poverty within his kingdom.* ¹⁵ *I saw that all who lived and walked under the sun followed the youth, the king's successor.* ¹⁶ *There was no end to all the people who were before them. But those who came later were not pleased with the successor. This too is meaningless, a chasing after the wind.*

> ¹ *Guard your steps when you go to the house of God. Go near to listen rather than to offer the sacrifice of fools, who do not know that they do wrong.*

> ² *Do not be quick with your mouth,*
> *do not be hasty in your heart*
> *to utter anything before God.*
> *God is in heaven*
> *and you are on earth,*
> *so let your words be few.*

Embracing Eternity IN THE HERE AND NOW

> *³ A dream comes when there are many cares,*
> *and many words mark the speech of a fool.*
>
> *⁴ When you make a vow to God, do not delay to fulfill it. He has no pleasure in fools; fulfill your vow. ⁵ It is better not to make a vow than to make one and not fulfill it. ⁶ Do not let your mouth lead you into sin. And do not protest to the temple messenger, "My vow was a mistake." Why should God be angry at what you say and destroy the work of your hands? ⁷ Much dreaming and many words are meaningless. Therefore fear God.*

I spent 27 years practicing a checklist Christianity. I convinced myself that if I wasn't committing any of the "major sins" and was present in church on Sundays, that would be enough for the Lord. I played the role of a good Christian girl pretty well. I had a lot of people convinced, even myself. I knew a lot about God. I could quote Bible verses, discuss theology, and even lead a few small groups. But I didn't have a relationship with the Lord; my heart was far from Him. I was simply going through the motions.

It wasn't until that day at lunch when my client asked where I saw God working in my life that I realized I was spiritually dead. I wanted all the benefits of a relationship with God without completely surrendering my life to Him. I lived both *in* the world and *of* it while trying to maintain the appearance of a good Christian. That double life led to constant inner conflict and turmoil, but all that changed when I handed the reins over to the Lord and surrendered my will to Him in *every* aspect. The Lord doesn't want divided hearts. He wants every part of us.

THE DANGERS OF A CHECKLIST CHRISTIANITY

WHAT DOES IT MEAN?

Ecclesiastes 5:1-7 calls us to approach God with reverence, giving the Lord our undivided worship. During Solomon's time, the temple was the place where God dwelt among His people. While churches today deserve respect and worship as they represent God's house, when Ecclesiastes was written, it was even more sacred as it held the presence of YAHWEH. Knowing that you are walking into the place where the Creator of the universe resided, should have changed the way the Israelites approached worship. Solomon observed that people outwardly acted like they were engaging in worship, but their hearts were far from their Heavenly Father.

Solomon identifies three potential pitfalls where humans are tempted to go through the motions rather than genuinely worship God. The first is through offerings. Our offerings and sacrifices are returned to the Lord with the acknowledgment that all is His in the first place. We shouldn't give our tithes, our first fruits, to gain the Lord's favor but out of a heart of gratitude. Second is our tendency to use prayers to manipulate God. Solomon admonishes us to listen first to what the Lord tells us before we ramble on about everything we need from the Lord. Yes, God desires to hear from His children, but he wants a relationship, not just transactional prayers to check a box.

Lastly, Solomon warns about the dangers of making a vow to the Lord. It can be tempting to bargain with God, but Scripture tells us that promises made to the Lord have severe terms (Deuteronomy 23:21-23). In your prayers, do not make promises to God that you know will be hard to keep, or once you receive what you've asked for, you fail to remember God's provision. These last verses want us to seriously consider the words we use when talking to the Lord. He takes no delight in the ramblings of fools who think their own words are more important than the word of God.

WHY DOES IT MATTER?

For those of us who have grown up in church, it can be easy to fall into the trap of just "going through the motions." We can say all the right things, we can quote Scripture, stay on top of Bible reading, and are sure to pray daily. But, a checklist Christianity is not what the Lord desires from his children. He wants your heart and your undivided attention because He alone is worthy of it!

This section of Ecclesiastes shines a light on the hypocrisy that plagues the church-you and I. We should heed these words as a warning and search our own hearts for signs of being whitewashed tombs (Matthew 23:27-28). How do we avoid being people who carelessly approach God? *We become good listeners.* God speaks to His children through His Word. The Bible is alive and active (Hebrews 4:12). But to know what the Lord is saying, we have to actually go to His Word. In the lives of believers, the Holy Spirit speaks to our hearts, guiding and directing our paths, but we must be quiet and attentive to its prompts. The book of Ecclesiastes is a constant reminder that as God's children we must not only hear God's words, but also apply them to our lives as He calls us to do. He formed us for this purpose.

We must be careful not to read these words from Solomon and take away that we should make our prayers short, and never make promises to the Lord. This is not what the text is saying. Instead of coming to the Lord first with our needs and wants, we need to open our hearts, ask the Lord to humble us, and grant us the mindset of

THE DANGERS OF A CHECKLIST CHRISTIANITY

Christ, as we align our desires with His. And, if you choose to speak a promise to the Lord, then make sure you have a plan to keep it! The Lord honors obedience and faithfulness.

THE HARD HEART WORK

The key takeaway from today's text is learning to listen to God and allowing His Word (the Bible) to shape our lives. Having a biblical worldview involves using Scripture to inform how you go about your day, the decisions you make, and the things you say yes to.

Think about your spiritual journey. Has your once sincere faith turned into a charade? What do you think has caused this shift?

How can you incorporate into each day time to restore and renew your faith?

Are you part of an accountability group? If not, is there a group of Christian women with whom you can study the Scriptures, share your struggles, and stir one another on in your faith?

True worship stems from inner heart transformation that leads to outward materialization.

PRAYER PROMPT

Heavenly Father, I ask that you search my heart, create in me a clean spirit, and renew my commitment to You. May I turn away from checkbox Christianity and genuinely pursue a relationship with you each day because we desire to know you more. In Jesus' Name, Amen.

Day 12
MONEY CAN'T BUY LASTING HAPPINESS

READ: Ecclesiastes 5:8-20

> ⁸ If you see the poor oppressed in a district, and justice and rights denied, do not be surprised at such things; for one official is eyed by a higher one, and over them both are others higher still. ⁹ The increase from the land is taken by all; the king himself profits from the fields.
>
> ¹⁰ Whoever loves money never has enough;
> whoever loves wealth is never satisfied with their income.
> This too is meaningless.
>
> ¹¹ As goods increase,
> so do those who consume them.
> And what benefit are they to the owners
> except to feast their eyes on them?
>
> ¹² The sleep of a laborer is sweet,
> whether they eat little or much,
> but as for the rich, their abundance
> permits them no sleep.
>
> ¹³ I have seen a grievous evil under the sun:
> wealth hoarded to the harm of its owners,

MONEY CAN'T BUY LASTING HAPPINESS

¹⁴ or wealth lost through some misfortune,
  so that when they have children
  there is nothing left for them to inherit.

¹⁵ Everyone comes naked from their mother's womb,
  and as everyone comes, so they depart.
  They take nothing from their toil
  that they can carry in their hands.

¹⁶ This too is a grievous evil:
  As everyone comes, so they depart,
  and what do they gain,
  since they toil for the wind?

¹⁷ All their days they eat in darkness,
  with great frustration, affliction and anger.

¹⁸ This is what I have observed to be good: that it is appropriate for a person to eat, to drink and to find satisfaction in their toilsome labor under the sun during the few days of life God has given them—for this is their lot. ¹⁹ Moreover, when God gives someone wealth and possessions, and the ability to enjoy them, to accept their lot and be happy in their toil—this is a gift of God. ²⁰ They seldom reflect on the days of their life, because God keeps them occupied with gladness of heart.

The ESPN Documentary "Broke" claims that over 70% of pro athletes go broke shortly after retiring. This seems pretty unfathomable, considering they were making millions upon millions. How does this happen? There are several explanations, but two of the most common reasons are they spend more than they make and their wealth is distributed to a lot of people.

Have you ever seen the sign that says, " You don't know how many friends you have until you own a beach house?" It's the same concept. I get it, early in my career, I had quick financial success, so much so that my whole outlook on money, possessions, and, eventually, my relationships shifted. However, God graciously showed me the damaging effect growing my wealth had on my family.

The attachment to my job as the source of my identity ran so deep that I had to physically walk away from that career. Through years of counseling and deep heart work, the Lord has repaired my relationship with my work, finances, and self-worth. Instead of money as a survival tool, it has become a lifeline for many of us. So, how do we learn to control our money and not let it control us?

WHAT DOES IT MEAN?

The last half of chapter five and the whole of chapter six will explore the many ways we work to acquire wealth and how, once again, the pursuit of money to satisfy is meaningless. Solomon shares seven ways we can be deceived by the false promise of fulfillment and security through money.

You never have enough; the more you make, the more you want (v10).

The more money consumption increases, the more people who hope to benefit from your wealth (v11).

Financial success ushers in anxiety over losing one's wealth (v12).

Hoarding wealth or a lack of generosity can harm relationships and ultimately wreak havoc on your soul (v13).

MONEY CAN'T BUY LASTING HAPPINESS

Wealth is easily lost, and many are one financial misfortune away from having nothing. What happens then (v14)?

When we die, anything we have acquired is left behind. What did we gain for all our work, sacrifice, and hustling (v15)?

After sharing Solomon's numerous observations about the pitfalls of placing our security, value, and identity in the amount of money in our bank account, Solomon invites us to turn to God and His gifts as a source of wealth. Everything we have comes from the Lord. It is when we rightfully acknowledge the good gifts from a loving Father that we can find joy in our work and take delight in the wealth and possessions given by the Lord. Solomon reminds us that financial success and material things are not the problem. If the Lord blesses you with these things, then enjoy them! But, be careful not to worship the created over the Creator and hold your possessions loosely. Our comfort, contentment, and cheer are not a product of God's blessings but a response to the One who so richly gives.

WHY DOES IT MATTER?

We've all heard the phrase, "You can't take it with you," or you "... don't see a U-Haul behind a hearse." Still, many of us wrestle with the "love of money." Jesus teaches often in the New Testament about the difficulties of a rich man (or the wealthy) going to Heaven (Matthew 19:24). It's not because having money prevents people from the Lord, but many are not willing to give up their lifestyle to follow Jesus.

But what happens when you finally get to the top, when you are the wealthiest person in the room, when you have everything you need and want, and then some, but you still feel empty? It is when we have it all but still feel the void that we begin to seek. This is where we begin a search for soul satisfaction, which is only found through Christ.

When we understand it's not just the things we have but the ability to enjoy those things from God, we can give generously and hold possessions loosely. God gives His children the gift of pleasure as another act of grace. The ability to laugh, feel loved, enjoy good food and fellowship on a sunny day is an act of God's grace to relieve the pain of life in a fallen world. So, whether you have little or a lot, all of it is the Lord's. We can enjoy it for our pleasure but should also use these gifts to benefit others.

THE HARD HEART WORK

I am not suggesting that you quit your job. But consider your relationship with money. Only you can answer these questions, so I encourage you to take time with the Lord and ask Him to reveal whether you are investing in the eternal or trying to keep up with the Joneses.

How would you describe how you feel when you have (or don't have) padding in your bank account?

Take a second to pull up your bank account. What do your spending habits say about what you value?

Now, considering our overflowing schedules, overstuffed closets, and over-the-top vacations, do we really *need* these things, or do we *want* them?

Make sure you control your money, or it will quickly control you.

MONEY CAN'T BUY LASTING HAPPINESS

LET'S PRAY

Heavenly Father, help me steward my resources well, both financially and in terms of where I spend my time. If something in my life has become an idol, please expose it and move me towards repentance. Help me stay focused on the eternal over the temporary. In Jesus' Name, Amen.

Day 13

MONEY WON'T BUY YOU EVERYTHING

READ: Ecclesiastes 6:1-12

¹ I have seen another evil under the sun, and it weighs heavily on mankind: ² God gives some people wealth, possessions and honor, so that they lack nothing their hearts desire, but God does not grant them the ability to enjoy them, and strangers enjoy them instead. This is meaningless, a grievous evil.

³ A man may have a hundred children and live many years; yet no matter how long he lives, if he cannot enjoy his prosperity and does not receive proper burial, I say that a stillborn child is better off than he. ⁴ It comes without meaning, it departs in darkness, and in darkness its name is shrouded. ⁵ Though it never saw the sun or knew anything, it has more rest than does that man— ⁶ even if he lives a thousand years twice over but fails to enjoy his prosperity. Do not all go to the same place?

⁷ Everyone's toil is for their mouth,
  yet their appetite is never satisfied.

⁸ What advantage have the wise over fools?
  What do the poor gain
  by knowing how to conduct themselves before others?

MONEY WON'T BUY YOU EVERYTHING

*⁹ Better what the eye sees
than the roving of the appetite.
This too is meaningless,
a chasing after the wind.*

*¹⁰ Whatever exists has already been named,
and what humanity is has been known;
no one can contend
with someone who is stronger.*

*¹¹ The more the words,
the less the meaning,
and how does that profit anyone?*

¹² For who knows what is good for a person in life, during the few and meaningless days they pass through like a shadow? Who can tell them what will happen under the sun after they are gone?

I was born in the eighties, so my high school years were spent laughing at the jokesters of Saturday Night Live. One of my favorite comedians during this time was Chris Farley. One night, between belly laughs, I remember looking at my dad and asking, "Do you think he was always this funny?"

A few months later, news broke that Farley died of an overdose at just 33 years old. His friends shared in the weeks that followed how Chris, while one of the most likable, funniest, and genuinely enjoyable guys to be around, often struggled with his quick rise to fame in Hollywood. Shortly before his death, Farley was quoted remarking on his popularity, "This notion of love is something that would be a wonderful thing. I don't think I've ever experienced it other than the love of my family. At this point, it's something beyond my grasp. But I can imagine it, and longing for it makes me sad."[3]

Here was a man who had it all from the world's standard, yet he still longed to be loved. I think about how many of us search for love, meaning, and someone to affirm our worthiness. The answer is right in front of us—Jesus. Yet, how often do we continue to look in other places?

WHAT DOES IT MEAN?

Solomon continues to explore the burden that money can bring to one's life. He opens chapter six, by telling of a man who has everything he could desire, not only wealth but status, yet, God doesn't allow him to enjoy them. His heart is never satisfied; he acquires a great fortune during his life, only to be turned over at his death for someone else's enjoyment. Solomon notes that this is a grievous evil at the end of verse two. I would have to agree. Man does not know why or who the Lord chooses to bless, but we should never expect or feel entitled to receive gifts from the Lord, and if we do, we should always receive them with a grateful heart.

We seek to acquire financial wealth, position, family, and health—but at what cost? In the following few verses, Solomon paints a bleak picture of what it looks like to gain material possessions at the expense of relationships. The man in these verses works his whole life but has no one to share it with. And upon his death, people fail to mourn him. Instead, they only care about his money. The same is

---

[3] *Chris Farley's Addiction Struggles*. Gratitude Lodge. (2024, March 22). https://www.gratitudelodge.com/chris-farley-addiction/

true of the fulfillment of our appetites. Life is an endless cycle: eat, sleep, work, and do it all over again tomorrow. This monotony, the redundancy of our days, causes us to ponder, "Is this all there is to life?" It is in that quest that we find God (Jeremiah 29:13).

In these last few verses, which examine the relationship between our work and life on earth, Solomon introduces two questions that will be answered in subsequent chapters. Who knows what is good for a person to do with their life? And who knows what will happen after they are gone? God alone has these answers.

WHY DOES IT MATTER?

We all know those people, the ones who have everything they could want but still seem to be miserable. How many times have we heard of a famous actor, musician, or political figure who took their life? And sometimes, it was by accident, an overdose. Yet, we still have to ask, outwardly, they had it all, what did they need to escape from?

"Money doesn't buy happiness, but I sure like to try!" says a friend, who jokes about her lack of funds. This friend is the opposite of the fool Solomon speaks of; she gives generously, at her expense, lives modestly, and would give you her shirt, shoes, and car if you asked. I think one of her spiritual gifts is the gift of poverty because she genuinely seems so detached from money. I wish that I had her laissez-faire approach to finances. But, the truth is, that's how she treats life. She understands Solomon's warnings to accept the gifts from God when they come and be grateful, but she doesn't depend on God's blessings to bring contentment. Her joy comes from knowing the Lord as Savior and her eternal hope as she considers God's character, past faithfulness, and future promises.

This prompts us to ask, if you can't enjoy life, what's the point of working at the expense of your family? If your goal is to be remembered, yet upon your death, people only care about what you left them, was all you gave up worth it? We spend so much time planning, calculating how to get ahead, and trying to control the future. If we are honest, sometimes we waste time trying to predict what God will do or figure out why He does this or that. But humans can't know the thoughts of God (1 Corinthians 2:11); his ways aren't ours (Isaiah 55:8-9). Thank goodness!

THE HARD HEART WORK

Death is the great equalizer.[4] The king, the peasant, the rich, the poor, the democrat, the republican, the made from scratch, the store-bought cupcake mom, death comes to us all.

How does knowing this reality and grasping this truth change how we live today?

Take some time today to write down things you have said yes to but that don't bring you joy. Do these fulfill the Lord's purpose for your life or have eternal significance?

Looking at the items you answered no to above, how can you work to remove them from your schedule?

What's the point of having it all if you don't have anyone to share it with?

---

[4] *Akin, D., & Akin PhD., J. (2016). Exalting Jesus in Ecclesiastes (Christ-Centered Exposition Commentary). Holman Reference.*

MONEY WON'T BUY YOU EVERYTHING

PRAYER PROMPT

Heavenly Father, I thank you for the abundant blessings in my life. Help me bring every detail of my life before you, meditating on the truth in Scripture and leaning into the Spirit's voice speaking to my heart. As I seek to honor you with work and relationships, help me hold the balance right. In Jesus' Name, Amen.

Day 14
HOW WILL YOUR LIFE BE REMEMBERED?

READ: Ecclesiastes: 7:1-14

*¹ A good name is better than fine perfume,
    and the day of death better than the day of birth.*

*² It is better to go to a house of mourning
    than to go to a house of feasting,
    for death is the destiny of everyone;
    the living should take this to heart.*

*³ Frustration is better than laughter,
    because a sad face is good for the heart.*

*⁴ The heart of the wise is in the house of mourning,
    but the heart of fools is in the house of pleasure.*

*⁵ It is better to heed the rebuke of a wise person
    than to listen to the song of fools.*

*⁶ Like the crackling of thorns under the pot,
    so is the laughter of fools.
    This too is meaningless.*

*⁷ Extortion turns a wise person into a fool,
    and a bribe corrupts the heart.*

HOW WILL YOUR LIFE BE REMEMBERED?

⁸ The end of a matter is better than its beginning,
*   and patience is better than pride.*

⁹ Do not be quickly provoked in your spirit,
*   for anger resides in the lap of fools.*

¹⁰ Do not say, "Why were the old days better than these?"
*   For it is not wise to ask such questions.*

¹¹ Wisdom, like an inheritance, is a good thing
*   and benefits those who see the sun.*

¹² Wisdom is a shelter
*   as money is a shelter,*
*   but the advantage of knowledge is this:*
*   Wisdom preserves those who have it.*

¹³ Consider what God has done:
*   Who can straighten*
*   what he has made crooked?*

¹⁴ When times are good, be happy;
*   but when times are bad, consider this:*
*   God has made the one*
*   as well as the other.*
*   Therefore, no one can discover*
*   anything about their future.*

A few years ago, a nearby acquaintance went to be with the Lord. When her family chose to remember her, they described her as a "Champion of the Gospel." Her life had a positive impact on so many people. There were numerous things they could have shared about her, yet these were the words they chose to remember her by.

Embracing Eternity IN THE HERE AND NOW

And not too long ago, a dear friend and spiritual mentor passed away unexpectedly. Our community felt her loss deeply. There weren't many people her life didn't touch. In her last conversation, she gently reminded me to choose love, even when it was hard. That's the kind of woman she was, both in word and deed. Her life pointed others to Christ.

These two ladies shared one thing: they lived with eternity in mind. Their lives and memories pointed others to Christ. I couldn't help but ask myself, how would my family and friends describe me? Would the words I encourage others with be evident in how I lived my life— or simply put, do I practice what I preach?

WHAT DOES IT MEAN?

The first seven verses draw attention to how we can live better today by fully embracing the reality of death. As Christians, we understand that death is not the end. It is the beginning of a new life. Even with this eternal perspective, losing a loved one is still painful. Solomon is not trying to brush over grief but encourages readers to turn to Jesus even in the midst of suffering. In verse one, Solomon speaks of the importance of a good reputation. What good is having numerous possessions if everyone thinks poorly of you? For the person who has walked in the ways of the Lord, their death can be a time of joyful remembrance, encouraging others to live in a way that positively impacts others.

The second half of this chapter details how someone can leave a legacy that points others to Christ. At a young age, Solomon asked for wisdom, which God granted, along with wealth and prosperity. And while Solomon walked in the ways of the Lord at times, he also

HOW WILL YOUR LIFE BE REMEMBERED?

engaged multiple times in open rebellion against the Lord's commands. Unfortunately, Solomon often lived by the "do as I say, not as I do" model instead of the "follow me as I follow Christ" model. While Solomon was still credited with being the wisest man who ever lived, his disobedience left a legacy of division and discord (the division of Israel upon his death in 1 Kings 11:29-32), that still affects the world today.

WHY DOES IT MATTER?

Solomon admonishes us to grasp Y.O.L.O (you only live once) in its entirety. You only get one life on earth; will you live it well and not waste it?

Are you going to squander it and invest in the fleeting? Are you falling victim to some of the things this world uses to distract us from walking with godly wisdom? Do you forsake relationships, hoard resources, and do whatever it takes to get ahead so that you can live your best life now? Do you sit around wishing you could return in time and relive your "glory days?" Maybe your temper runs hot, your patience is thin, and you always look ahead and never enjoy the present.

If we glean from the Preacher's wisdom and exhortation to live with the end in sight, there will be eternal rewards, but we can also experience benefits now. As John Mark Comer shares in his book *Practicing the Way*, "Jesus didn't just come to die; he came to live." Live as if each day could be your last, making the most of every opportunity and focusing on the things that matter for eternity, not the ones that wither away.

THE HARD HEART WORK

Hopefully, you've had the opportunity to know someone whose light shone brightly for Jesus. Their love for the Lord was contagious, and their lives were clearly marked by hope and joy.

Today, Solomon's words should persuade us to ask, "When we die, how will we be remembered?"

What words or phrases would you hope someone might use to describe your life?

We don't know when our lives will end, so how should that reality change how we live today?

Since Jesus is the only name that will transcend eternity, let us leave a lasting legacy that points to Christ.

PRAYER PROMPT

Heavenly Father, as Your child, I know death has lost its sting. When I leave this world, I will be in Your holy presence. But this side of eternity, death is still difficult to walk through. Help me see your grace and mercy through suffering, and above all, guide me as we aim to live worthy of the gospel. In Jesus' Name. Amen.

Day 15
SERENITY TO ACCEPT THE THINGS WE CANNOT CHANGE

READ: Ecclesiastes: 7:15-29

> ^{15} In this meaningless life of mine I have seen both of these:
> the righteous perishing in their righteousness,
> and the wicked living long in their wickedness.
>
> ^{16} Do not be overrighteous,
> neither be overwise—
> why destroy yourself?
>
> ^{17} Do not be overwicked,
> and do not be a fool—
> why die before your time?
>
> ^{18} It is good to grasp the one
> and not let go of the other.
> Whoever fears God will avoid all extremes.
>
> ^{19} Wisdom makes one wise person more powerful
> than ten rulers in a city.
>
> ^{20} Indeed, there is no one on earth who is righteous,
> no one who does what is right and never sins.

Embracing Eternity IN THE HERE AND NOW

²¹ Do not pay attention to every word people say,
   or you may hear your servant cursing you—

²² for you know in your heart
   that many times you yourself have cursed others.

²³ All this I tested by wisdom and I said,
   "I am determined to be wise"—
   but this was beyond me.

²⁴ Whatever exists is far off and most profound—
   who can discover it?

²⁵ So I turned my mind to understand,
   to investigate and to search out wisdom and the scheme of things
   and to understand the stupidity of wickedness
   and the madness of folly.

²⁶ I find more bitter than death
   the woman who is a snare,
   whose heart is a trap
   and whose hands are chains.
   The man who pleases God will escape her,
   but the sinner she will ensnare.

²⁷ "Look," says the Teacher, "this is what I have discovered:
   "Adding one thing to another to discover the scheme of things—

²⁸ while I was still searching
   but not finding—
   I found one upright man among a thousand,
   but not one upright woman among them all.

SERENITY TO ACCEPT THE THINGS WE CANNOT CHANGE

> *²⁹ This only have I found:*
> *God created mankind upright,*
> *but they have gone in search of many schemes."*

The first time I went horseback riding, an instructor rode with me. I was so nervous that I gripped the reins too tightly, and the leather began to blister my skin. Seeing my inability to enjoy the experience, the instructor reminded me I could soften my grip because she was there and could steer the horse back on track or step in and take over if needed. I loosened my grip with much reluctance but found freedom. Once I released a bit of assumed control, the experience was much more enjoyable.

I can't help but think about that illustration as it relates to our relationship with God. He's always there, watching over, guiding, and directing us, yet we desire to be in control. So we hold on tight, trying to manipulate and maneuver our way through life. I've lost count of the messes I've made trying to usurp God's plan, impatiently moving in my strength instead of waiting on the Lord and allowing Him to work.

WHAT DOES IT MEAN?

In verse 15, Solomon asks why bad things happen to good people and why good things happen to bad people. Recall in the previous two verses how Solomon acknowledges, and seems to accept the sovereignty of God. He comments that humans can't undo the work of God. He instructs when times are good we should give God praise, and when they are bad, we still give God praise—because God is the author of both. Solomon spends a great deal of time trying to comprehend why the Lord acts the way He does, but he always turns back to the humble submission that God is God. Solomon is not. These exchanges should be encouraging for us, as it is expected for us to wrestle with God. Our Father understands we will struggle to accept the things we don't deem as fair or right. Ultimately, we must trust that God's ways are better and more faithful. He will fulfill His plan (Ephesians 1:11).

Solomon concludes this chapter by making a few observations about what it means to live a righteous life. The virtuous person is one who "fears God" (v18). We can't answer why God chooses to end the life of a godly person and allow an evil man to live on—only He controls life and death. However, we can control our responses and actions. We should keep a heart of humility, guarding against thinking too highly of ourselves and leaning on our own strength. A natural benefit of walking in biblical wisdom is the ability to make good decisions, which brings about positive outcomes.

WHY DOES IT MATTER?

For the fifth week in a row, I plopped down on the couch in my pastor's office, my Bible filled with sticky notes, question marks, and bleeding with *all* the highlighter colors. Simply put, I was trying to figure out God. Don't misunderstand; we are called to know God, learn of His character, meditate on His love letter to us (the Bible), and pray to Him. But I wasn't trying to know God. I was frustrated because I felt like God left me out of the loop. I was irritated. He didn't consult me or fill me in on what He was doing.

Solomon speaks to this frustration: the quest for man to understand God in a way we weren't meant to. God is the Creator; we are creation. As such, He has the final say on what He chooses to reveal

SERENITY TO ACCEPT THE THINGS WE CANNOT CHANGE

to us. And that's a good thing. Would He be the omnipotent God if we were able to figure Him out? We don't want the Creator of the universe to be on our level and equal with mankind. Humans are fickle; we talk from both sides of our mouths, change our minds on a whim, and half the time, we just make it up as we go. But our God, He is all-knowing, all-powerful, all-present, never-changing, and eternal, to name a few.[5] It is a meaningless pursuit spending our time trying to answer questions that only God can. It is the source of the first sin in the Garden of Eden, the quest to be like God (Genesis 3:3). When we release to God the need to control, the desire to have all the answers, and to be responsible for the outcome, we give ourselves breathing room. It's not about us. Find freedom in that statement. We don't have to live perfect lives, but let our lives point to a perfect God.

THE HARD HEART WORK

Faith is having confidence in what we can't see. In a world where very little is left to the imagination, accepting and agreeing that God's ways are better can be challenging, especially when we can't visibly see Him working.

What area in your life do you need to loosen your grip?

Is there something beyond your control? Have you spent many sleepless nights plagued by worry, doubt, and anxiousness?

---

[5] *Wilkin, J. (2016). None Like Him: 10 Ways God Is Different from US (and Why That's a Good Thing). Crossway.*

Embracing Eternity IN THE HERE AND NOW

How does knowing that God is in ultimate control and we are just stewards of the things in our lives, help you release your concerns to God?

God can't always be explained, but He can be known.

PRAYER PROMPT

Heavenly Father, instead of me working tirelessly to be like You, let me find rest in Who You are. Lord, help me to stop clinging so tightly to things beyond my control, placing our confidence in you because you are faithful. In Jesus' Name, Amen.

Day 16

SUBMISSION EVEN WHEN IT'S HARD

READ: Ecclesiastes 8

*¹ Who is like the wise?
   Who knows the explanation of things?
   A person's wisdom brightens their face
   and changes its hard appearance.*

² Obey the king's command, I say, because you took an oath before God. ³ Do not be in a hurry to leave the king's presence. Do not stand up for a bad cause, for he will do whatever he pleases. ⁴ Since a king's word is supreme, who can say to him, "What are you doing?"

*⁵ Whoever obeys his command will come to no harm,
   and the wise heart will know the proper time and procedure.*

*⁶ For there is a proper time and procedure for every matter,
   though a person may be weighed down by misery.*

*⁷ Since no one knows the future,
   who can tell someone else what is to come?*

*⁸ As no one has power over the wind to contain it,
   so no one has power over the time of their death.*

Embracing Eternity IN THE HERE AND NOW

> *As no one is discharged in time of war,*
> *so wickedness will not release those who practice it.*

⁹ *All this I saw, as I applied my mind to everything done under the sun. There is a time when a man lords it over others to his own hurt.* ¹⁰ *Then too, I saw the wicked buried—those who used to come and go from the holy place and receive praise in the city where they did this. This too is meaningless.*

¹¹ *When the sentence for a crime is not quickly carried out, people's hearts are filled with schemes to do wrong.* ¹² *Although a wicked person who commits a hundred crimes may live a long time, I know that it will go better with those who fear God, who are reverent before him.* ¹³ *Yet because the wicked do not fear God, it will not go well with them, and their days will not lengthen like a shadow.*

¹⁴ *There is something else meaningless that occurs on earth: the righteous who get what the wicked deserve, and the wicked who get what the righteous deserve. This too, I say, is meaningless.* ¹⁵ *So I commend the enjoyment of life, because there is nothing better for a person under the sun than to eat and drink and be glad. Then joy will accompany them in their toil all the days of the life God has given them under the sun.*

¹⁶ *When I applied my mind to know wisdom and to observe the labor that is done on earth—people getting no sleep day or night—* ¹⁷ *then I saw all that God has done. No one can comprehend what goes on under the sun. Despite all their efforts to search it out, no one can discover its meaning. Even if the wise claim they know, they cannot really comprehend it.*

I'll never forget the day I told my parents, " I can't wait to be 18! I am going to say and do whatever I want!"

SUBMISSION EVEN WHEN IT'S HARD

They responded smirkingly, "Well, we look forward to seeing how that turns out for you."

I longed to escape my parents' rule; autonomy was my greatest desire. Once out on my own, I learned flying solo wasn't all I thought it would be. I also quickly unearthed that submission is a lifetime affair. If we are not yielding to human authority, then we are yielding to the Lord's. There really is not a reality where we can abstain from all measures of subordination. And as we rack up more trips around the sun, we may believe we have more freedom to respond and act individualistically. However, our choices and behavior always have consequences.

Some seem to have little or no desire to rebel against the rules. But if you are one of those who have to put your hand on the stove to believe it's hot, you are my people. Maybe for you, like me, it's not necessarily the rules that cause you to buck but those who enforce those rules. On numerous occasions, I find myself questioning their abilities. What gives them the right? Who do they think they are? Or, probably the boldest assumption—I should be in that position.

We can say we are stubborn, strong-willed, or independent, but the truth is—it is pride. How do we learn to submit to the physical and divine authority in our lives?

WHAT DOES IT MEAN?

The overall theme in this chapter is submission to authority, both secular and sacred. In verses 2-9, Solomon focuses his attention on earthly government, addressing the expectation of our behavior in the presence of the king (or people who preside over us).

Embracing Eternity IN THE HERE AND NOW

It is prudent to submit to worldly authorities when appropriate and at the proper time (v 5-6), remembering that those who govern us on this side of eternity are granted power that is restrained. Despite outward appearance, earthly rulers are under the authority of the sovereign God. One day, they will account for their deeds in the flesh (2 Corinthians 5:10). Therefore, they must rule with biblical wisdom, avoiding commands that counter God's Word and governing with respect and love. But we know that doesn't often happen. Power is corrupted, leading rulers to take advantage of, and even inflict harm upon, those in their jurisdiction.

In verses 10-17, Solomon transfers focus from men's authority to God's authority. He highlights that, for some, this may cause frustration. Why might we struggle to exist under the authority of a good God? Because our limited human understanding will fail to comprehend the complexities of our omnipotent God. There will be times when we are tempted to consider God's divine rule as good compared to the "abundance" of injustice in the world. Why do the evil get the reward of the righteous, and why do the righteous receive the consequences of the evil? No one knows except for the divine ruler. And yes, these determinations can seem "unfair" on this side of eternity, but we will make ourselves miserable trying to play God (Isaiah 55:8-9). Solomon concludes this chapter with further exhortation that we must live for more than just the here and now. One day, the morally bankrupt will get what they deserve, and the righteous will be victorious over the effects of sin.

WHY DOES THIS MATTER?

Have you ever had a problem with authority? Before you respond, remember that, though you may not have openly rebelled against leadership, snide comments to a friend or ill-meaning thoughts potentially undermine authority. At some point in our lives, we have all contested those in power. Whether it was a parent, a boss, an organization director, a church pastor, or the president of the United States, our natural response (in most cases) isn't acceptance but rejection of the rule.

Our opinionated elitism is nothing new. It stems from the curse attached to Eve in the Garden of Eden. We see her desire for self-autonomy repeatedly played out in our own lives. Yet, Solomon admonishes us to (wisely) embrace those in power over us. How do we do this? We need to know the appropriate time to submit and when it is proper to resist. Divine rule always trumps human rule. If someone in authority is asking you to do something that goes against God's Word, as Christians, we must follow the Lord's commands before the orders of men.

It can be tempting to turn away from God when we see the injustice around us. Or, when "inequity" appears in our own lives, we can believe we've been dealt a bad hand. But we must remember that our view is obstructed; we only see a tiny sliver (or vapor) of the picture. God, who was here from the beginning, knows the whole story—from start to finish. We must trust in Him. When we find it difficult to believe, we must ask the Holy Spirit to help us in our unbelief (Mark 9:24).

THE HARD HEART WORK

Many years have passed since my 18-year-old self made that naive declaration. The wisdom gained during those years has taught me just because you can say or do whatever you want, that does not equate to right thinking. Take some time today and pray that the Lord will give you the strength to show honor and respect to those he placed in governing authority over your life.

Is there a relationship in which you struggle to submit to their leadership?

Barring abuse of power like discussed above, have you rejected the authority God has placed in your life?

Is practicing biblical submission something you grapple with? If so, write down a couple of ways you work towards surrendering to authority in your life.

Knowing that God is the ultimate authority, we can submit to earthly leadership even when we don't agree, understand, or question their actions.

PRAYER PROMPT

Heavenly Father, I ask that you help me to yield to the authority you have placed in my life even when I disagree, find it difficult, and struggle to understand their direction. Give me peace as I know that submission to those You ordain is ultimately submission to You. In Jesus' Name, Amen.

Day 17

EMBRACING EACH DAY AS A GIFT

READ: Ecclesiastes 9

¹ *So I reflected on all this and concluded that the righteous and the wise and what they do are in God's hands, but no one knows whether love or hate awaits them.* ² *All share a common destiny—the righteous and the wicked, the good and the bad, the clean and the unclean, those who offer sacrifices and those who do not.*

As it is with the good,
  so with the sinful;
  as it is with those who take oaths,
  so with those who are afraid to take them.

³ *This is the evil in everything that happens under the sun: The same destiny overtakes all. The hearts of people, moreover, are full of evil and there is madness in their hearts while they live, and afterward they join the dead.* ⁴ *Anyone who is among the living has hope—even a live dog is better off than a dead lion!*

⁵ *For the living know that they will die,*
  but the dead know nothing;

they have no further reward,
and even their name is forgotten.

6 Their love, their hate
and their jealousy have long since vanished;
never again will they have a part
in anything that happens under the sun.

7 Go, eat your food with gladness, and drink your wine with a joyful heart, for God has already approved what you do. **8** Always be clothed in white, and always anoint your head with oil. **9** Enjoy life with your wife, whom you love, all the days of this meaningless life that God has given you under the sun— all your meaningless days. For this is your lot in life and in your toilsome labor under the sun. **10** Whatever your hand finds to do, do it with all your might, for in the realm of the dead, where you are going, there is neither working nor planning nor knowledge nor wisdom.

11 I have seen something else under the sun:
The race is not to the swift
or the battle to the strong,
nor does food come to the wise
or wealth to the brilliant
or favor to the learned;
but time and chance happen to them all.

12 Moreover, no one knows when their hour will come:
As fish are caught in a cruel net,
or birds are taken in a snare,
so people are trapped by evil times
that fall unexpectedly upon them.

13 I also saw under the sun this example of wisdom that greatly impressed me: **14** There was once a small city with only a few

EMBRACING EACH DAY AS A GIFT

people in it. And a powerful king came against it, surrounded it and built huge siege works against it. **15** *Now there lived in that city a man poor but wise, and he saved the city by his wisdom. But nobody remembered that poor man.* **16** *So I said, "Wisdom is better than strength." But the poor man's wisdom is despised, and his words are no longer heeded.*

17 *The quiet words of the wise are more to be heeded than the shouts of a ruler of fools.*

18 *Wisdom is better than weapons of war, but one sinner destroys much good.*

It's always a shot to the heart when we hear of a loved one diagnosed with a terminal illness or the news of a young person's abrupt passing appears in your messages. While coping with the reality of imminent mortality is never easy, there are two times in my life when the Lord used the unanticipated ending of a life to arrest my attention.

The first occurred when I was a freshman in high school. Someone I knew, someone my own age, suddenly died. Tony was fourteen years old, and just two weeks before school started, he was killed in a car crash. Although I did not know him very well, the news of his death shook me. Fourteen was too young; people just do not die at fourteen. I briefly pondered what would happen to me if I were to die that day. However, as usual, I soon turned my attention back to my hair, clothes, or writing a note to a friend. After all, I planned on living until the ripe old age of one hundred, so I figured there was plenty of time for me to worry about my own mortality.

Later, in college, I received a call that my uncle, only thirty-four years old, had passed away just six months after receiving the daunting news that he had cancer. Again, I thought that he was too young, and in the prime of life with a promising career, a lovely wife, a new home, and two adorable young children. He was so young. I am in my late thirties and feel like life is just really beginning. With this perspective, it is hard to believe anything other than there remains lots of living still ahead.

No doubt every one of us has experienced the shock of learning the life of someone we knew was cut short. In our current medically advanced culture, unless someone lives to be one hundred, it seems that all lives are short-lived, no matter what age individuals are taken in death. This should prompt us to ask: are we treating each day as a gift, as if it could be our last?

WHAT DOES IT MEAN?

Ecclesiastes echoes the same themes, sentiments, and phrases so repetitively that it can tempt us to say, "I get it, Solomon, let's move on." But we actually don't get it. We are fickle and easily distracted. This is why Solomon reiterates his observations and words of wisdom from earlier in the following four chapters. Solomon's final assertions aim to remind readers that we can only find meaning in this life through God. As discussed, death is the great equalizer. The crooked and the virtuous suffer the same fate. The difference is where they will spend eternity. Life is unpredictable. Even the most prepared, well-studied, and plan-driven people can't control the outcomes.

Chapter nine reinforces a few realities from previous chapters. Death is going to come to us all. As much as we try, humans can't explain or exhaustively understand God. Tomorrow doesn't come with a guarantee, so capitalize on today. We know we aren't the author of time and our days are numbered, yet how we live our lives suggests otherwise. Solomon understood this reality and wrote Ecclesiastes to "smash into tiny pieces that we can be like God."[6] There's nothing new under the sun, not even our desire for equality for God. It was the original sin in Eden and one that continues to plague mankind.

As stated in the scripture passage for today, life has advantages over death (v 4). Those who are gone from this world have no further opportunity to accept Christ. Their eternal fate is already sealed. But, for those still living, each day is an opportunity to turn to Jesus as Lord and Savior. Death is inevitable, but that doesn't mean we can't enjoy life on earth. Solomon encourages us to eat our food with gladness, enjoy time with our companions, and work with all our might because God delights seeing His children enjoy the gifts he bestows on them! So, while we live with eternity in mind, let's cherish the gift of the present, too!

WHY DOES IT MATTER?

Solomon's main motivation for writing Ecclesiastes was to exhort his readers to live sagely. He wanted us to seek out that which has eternal significance and stop trying to exhaust ourselves with pursuits that never satisfy. He desired that we measure our choices based on the questions: "What's the point of all this? If I die tomorrow, what will it matter?" While we prefer to avoid thoughts like this, they are necessary. I understand it is a hard truth to

---

[6] *Gibson, D. (2017). Living Life Backward: How Ecclesiastes Teaches Us to Live in Light of the End. Crossway.*

swallow, but avoiding death, not talking about it, and refusing to acknowledge our fate won't prevent the inevitable.

Solomon did not offer these sentiments to evoke defeatism. Instead, he shared these observations to offer eternal hope. He wanted to show us that our lives today can be better when we exist for eternity. When we focus on Jesus, we are freed from the burden of substantiating the importance of life. It's unnecessary to hustle or drive ourselves into the ground to find our purpose. We can stop filling our spaces with more "stuff" to feel satisfied. Instead, we can make the most of our time today by having a relationship with the Lord and living for an eternity where we will experience the absence of sin.

The Lord appoints when our life begins and ends. While we are still breathing, He has work for us to do. The harvest is plentiful, and we were designed to know God and make Him known (Matthew 9:35-38). Each day, we have an opportunity to share the gospel and tell of the eternal hope found in Christ. While we are speaking of the good news, with gratitude, we can enjoy the gifts of time spent with family gathered around a good meal, laughing, and celebrating all that the Lord has done for us today and for all eternity!

THE HARD HEART WORK

The phrase "live like tomorrow was your last day" often gets thrown around to encourage people to think about making the most of life. While I understand the sentiment, might I suggest we take Tim McGraw's advice and " live like you are dying?" Because, well, the reality is, we all are wasting away (2 Corinthians 4:16). If tomorrow

EMBRACING EACH DAY AS A GIFT

were your last day, you might be tempted to abandon all responsibilities and hunker down with those you hold dear.

However, this isn't a practical way to live on a day-to-day basis. In light of this, if you looked over your priorities, specifically where you spent your time and money, what story would they tell?

Did you intentionally spend time serving, showing people love, and sharing the gospel?

How can you incorporate living with an eternal perspective into your life each month, week, and day?

Embrace each day as a gift and make the most of every opportunity to share the gospel and show the world around you the love of Jesus.

LET'S PRAY

Heavenly Father, I thank you for the gift of earthly and eternal life. Help me to enjoy the present as a gift while acknowledging that one day, I will stand before you and give an account of my actions on earth. Guide me as we live each day for You. In Jesus' name, Amen.

Day 18

TRUSTING GOD WHEN IT DOESN'T MAKE SENSE

READ: Ecclesiastes 10

*¹ As dead flies give perfume a bad smell,
    so a little folly outweighs wisdom and honor.*

*² The heart of the wise inclines to the right,
    but the heart of the fool to the left.*

*³ Even as fools walk along the road,
    they lack sense
    and show everyone how stupid they are.*

*⁴ If a ruler's anger rises against you,
    do not leave your post;
    calmness can lay great offenses to rest.*

*⁵ There is an evil I have seen under the sun,
    the sort of error that arises from a ruler:*

*⁶ Fools are put in many high positions,
    while the rich occupy the low ones.*

*⁷ I have seen slaves on horseback,
    while princes go on foot like slaves.*

TRUSTING GOD WHEN IT DOESN'T MAKE SENSE

⁸ Whoever digs a pit may fall into it;
  whoever breaks through a wall may be bitten by a snake.

⁹ Whoever quarries stones may be injured by them;
  whoever splits logs may be endangered by them.

¹⁰ If the ax is dull
  and its edge unsharpened,
  more strength is needed,
  but skill will bring success.

¹¹ If a snake bites before it is charmed,
  the charmer receives no fee.

¹² Words from the mouth of the wise are gracious,
  but fools are consumed by their own lips.

¹³ At the beginning their words are folly;
  at the end they are wicked madness—

¹⁴ and fools multiply words.
  No one knows what is coming—
  who can tell someone else what will happen after them?

¹⁵ The toil of fools wearies them;
  they do not know the way to town.

¹⁶ Woe to the land whose king was a servant
  and whose princes feast in the morning.

¹⁷ Blessed is the land whose king is of noble birth
  and whose princes eat at a proper time—
  for strength and not for drunkenness.

¹⁸ Through laziness, the rafters sag;
  because of idle hands, the house leaks.

¹⁹ A feast is made for laughter,
 wine makes life merry,
 and money is the answer for everything.

²⁰ Do not revile the king even in your thoughts,
 or curse the rich in your bedroom,
 because a bird in the sky may carry your words,
 and a bird on the wing may report what you say.

Driving down the road, my daughter, without warning, threw some theological curveballs my way. "Why did God create humans if He knew they would sin? Why do bad things happen if God controls everything? If God loves people, why do some people go to Hell?"

Her questions were not without merit. I have a lot of questions, too. There are numerous precepts in the Bible I can't understand and struggle to accept by mere faith.

I can easily recall the day I went to my pastor and shared how I found it challenging to accept hard truths in Scripture.

"You know, you would make a really good atheist," he responded.

Not exactly the words you hope to hear from your spiritual mentor. It's difficult to police our thoughts when they start down the "what-if," "why," or "how could you," rabbit hole, demanding answers to things we may never fully understand this side of eternity. God invites and expects us to question. He is not upset by wrestling. He understands our doubts. But, ultimately, we have a choice to make. Either we believe what God says is true, or we don't. I pray that through faith, we can all learn to accept God is in control and His ways are better than ours.

TRUSTING GOD WHEN IT DOESN'T MAKE SENSE

WHAT DOES IT MEAN?

This chapter offers multiple insights into the reality of life in a fallen world. Corrupt leaders will be put in positions of authority, power will be abused, the righteous will be overlooked, and life, at least from our human perspective, is unfair. Solomon is exploring the question many of us ask: Why is God allowing evil to prevail?"

Solomon also draws our attention to the fact that we can do everything "right," and our lives can still be filled with sorrow, struggle, and strife. Conversely, someone else might be doing everything "wrong," and their life is prosperous, plentiful, and pleasant. There will be many times we seek answers from God that He chooses to not reveal to His children. The earthly success of wicked men while the righteous experience suffering is something that will remain a paradox on this side of eternity. But Scripture affirms one day the Lord, the ultimate judge, will punish evil and good will prevail.

Through faith, Solomon realized that God can be trusted, regardless of what He has planned for His people, even when we don't understand His ways. Solomon praised the Lord for being His Savior and strength, even during his darkest moments.

WHY DOES IT MATTER?

The last few chapters of Ecclesiastes recapitulate that we are incapable of fully understanding the ways of the Lord. Solomon repeatedly draws attention to the fact that good things happen to bad people, and bad things happen to good people. It is a meaningless task to dissect and ponder the "why" behind many of life's injustices. For us, the seeming unfairness of life can cause us to question the goodness of God, yet Solomon's words are echoed in 1 Corinthians 1:27, " But God chose the foolish things of the world to shame the wise; God chose the weak things of the world to shame the strong."

Believers belong to an "upside down kingdom" where "blessed are the poor in spirit, (Matthew 5:3)" "the first will be last, and the last will be first (Matthew 19:30)." And, above all else, we are to think more highly of others than ourselves. For the Christian, our lives should be so radically countercultural that people can't help but ask about our source of peace, contentment, and joy, even in this broken world. As we read Solomon's counsel, we are reminded that God often works in ways we humans can't understand. But, we can call on the Lord and ask the Holy Spirit to help illuminate our hearts and minds so that we may become wise through Christ. Further, good news and assurance exist for those attempting to walk in His ways. Even when we wander away or act carelessly, we can't thwart God's plan—His purposes will always come to pass.

THE HARD HEART WORK

I mentioned that we live in an "upside-down kingdom." What do you think that means? Jot down a few examples from *The Beatitudes*, found in Matthew 5:1-12, of how Jesus calls us to live in a manner that contradicts the messages touted by the world.

Do you ever struggle to keep your faith when you can't see God at work?

2 Corinthians 4:18 says, "So we fix our eyes not on what is seen, but on what is unseen since what is seen is temporary, but what is

unseen is eternal." Take some time today and write this verse on a sticky note, on your mirror, or make a screensaver.

How does focusing on the eternal help us accept things we don't understand?

No matter what God has planned for His people, God can be trusted, even when we don't understand His ways.

PRAYER PROMPT

Heavenly Father, I surrender the need to have all the answers over to You. I trust that Your ways are better than my ways. I come to you with a heavy heart; there is so much evil in the world. Help me remember You see me, care for me, and have a plan more extraordinary than anything I can imagine. Help me to trust and obey even when I don't understand. In Jesus' Name, Amen.

Day 19

FLOURISHING IN THE WAITING

READ: Ecclesiastes 11

> ¹ Ship your grain across the sea;
>   after many days you may receive a return.
>
> ² Invest in seven ventures, yes, in eight;
>   you do not know what disaster may come upon the land.
>
> ³ If clouds are full of water,
>   they pour rain on the earth.
>   Whether a tree falls to the south or to the north,
>   in the place where it falls, there it will lie.
>
> ⁴ Whoever watches the wind will not plant;
>   whoever looks at the clouds will not reap.
>
> ⁵ As you do not know the path of the wind,
>   or how the body is formed in a mother's womb,
>   so you cannot understand the work of God,
>   the Maker of all things.
>
> ⁶ Sow your seed in the morning,
>   and at evening let your hands not be idle,
>   for you do not know which will succeed,

> *whether this or that,*
> *or whether both will do equally well.*
>
> *⁷ Light is sweet,*
> *and it pleases the eyes to see the sun.*
>
> *⁸ However many years anyone may live,*
> *let them enjoy them all.*
> *But let them remember the days of darkness,*
> *for there will be many.*
> *Everything to come is meaningless.*
>
> *⁹ You who are young, be happy while you are young,*
> *and let your heart give you joy in the days of your youth.*
> *Follow the ways of your heart*
> *and whatever your eyes see,*
> *but know that for all these things*
> *God will bring you into judgment.*
>
> *¹⁰ So then, banish anxiety from your heart*
> *and cast off the troubles of your body,*
> *for youth and vigor are meaningless.*

A few years ago, a friend shared with me about a woman in her church who recently passed away. She battled cancer for numerous years, fully understanding her days were numbered.

The woman contemplated buying new living room furniture for years but dismissed the notion as frivolous. Unsure of how much longer she had until she would go to her eternal home, she decided to make the most of her earthly digs and purchase the pieces she'd had been considering. Unfortunately, not long after she made these purchases, she passed away. A few weeks after her death, the furniture arrived to her very shocked family. She never told them she ordered the pieces. While their wife and mother moved into a room in her Father's house, these final purchases served as a sweet daily reminder for those who remained behind.

This story has always stuck with me. It is such a tangible reminder of life's fragility. We flippantly spout, "life is short," but do we really meditate on the implications of the phrase? We know how uncertain life is, but how often do we make plans for the future without considering we may never see tomorrow?

WHAT DOES IT MEAN?

How do we flourish knowing we will one day cease to exist? Chapter eleven encourages us to invest in various ventures, be bold, take chances, and try new things. And since we can't take our wealth or possessions with us, our lives should be marked by generosity. This call to liberally share with others isn't relegated to just our finances. Our gifts, talents, time, and services are also to be an abundant offering to others.

The last verses of chapter eleven embody the thematic message of Ecclesiastes: both life and death exist yet we can experience joy and live in the face of judgment simultaneously. Solomon urges us to appreciate life, especially when we are young, because one day, our hair will gray, our health will deteriorate, and ultimately we will pass away. Some versions of verse eight use the word futile or fleeting— driving home the point that our time in the light (earthly life) pales in comparison to our time in darkness (death).[7] Keeping that reality

---

[7] *Akin, D., & Akin PhD., J. (2016). Exalting Jesus in Ecclesiastes (Christ-Centered Exposition Commentary). Holman Reference.*

in mind, don't delay. Cherish your life today. Stop with the "one-days," "when I or when my children," and "sometime real soon." We are not promised the future, so start living now!

Solomon shares with us the secret to relishing the here and now. He calls us to experience this earth the way God intended His creation to interact with it. It is not that life under the sun is meaningless, but a life devoid of God is trivial. God's Word is the divine instruction manual outlining how we should live. We are to use the resources and talents the way God intended, not abusing them for our own pleasure. We are to "banish anxiety from our hearts and cast off the troubles of our body." This is how we find enjoyment in life. Solomon further proves that we can keep an eternal perspective while still living in the present moment. We must resist the urge to idolize the past or glamorize our future. Each day is a gift from a gracious God. Each day, we commit and sacrifice to the Lord as we find pleasure in life under the sun.

WHY DOES IT MATTER?

Solomon is telling us to avoid "the paralysis of analysis."[8] Sometimes, we can be so immobilized by fear, worrying we will make the wrong decision, or projecting all the possible outcomes that we just shut down. As believers in Christ, we don't have to worry because God is in ultimate control, and nothing we can do will thwart His divine plan for the world. That doesn't mean there won't be earthly

---

[8] *TGC Course: Introduction to Ecclesiastes. The Gospel Coalition. (n.d.).* https://www.thegospelcoalition.org/course/ecclesiastes/

consequences for actions, but there's freedom in knowing we aren't that powerful. We can't change the trajectory of mankind. Woohoo!

Humanity tends to sit in two camps: life is short, so I will do whatever I want; or focus so much on the afterlife that I miss out on the gift of the present. Billy Joel sings, "Only the good die young." With this philosophy, people embrace all the pleasures of life to an extreme measure. They live in the here and now with reckless abandon and no consideration for the future. On the other hand, those attempting to heed Solomon's advice have a death grip (literally) on life and are so consumed with living for eternity that they don't enjoy any of God's good gifts today. Both of these two extremes should be avoided. Solomon tells us in chapter eleven that God is both the author of life on earth and eternity. He desires His children to find enjoyment in both.

These parallel truths present a tension in our broken world. How do we enjoy our lives today as we prepare for eternity? We take Solomon's words to heart and enjoy God's gifts, sharing with others and always remembering the source of our blessings. While we are young and our bodies still work (minus a few bumps and bruises), we are to enjoy the days of our youth because one day they will be gone. We either age or depart from this earth. But, friends, even though our bodies experience the effects of sin as we grow older, remember that for the believer, our light momentary affliction is nothing compared to the eternal weight of glory (and new bodies) we have in Heaven (2 Corinthians 4:17-18).

FLOURISHING IN THE WAITING

THE HARD HEART WORK

Even those who resist the urge to spend every dollar fighting the outward effects of aging cannot avoid the mental toll getting older can have on us all. Accepting the reality that we can't do things we once did or learning new limitations is disheartening.

Ecclesiastes 11 poses the question, "How can I have joy in the face of aging and death?"[9] What would your response be?

Do you wrestle with growing older? How can you learn to accept and enjoy "aging well?"

How can you find joy in your present circumstances, not living in the past, nor wishing away tomorrow, but find true contentment in the gift of the present?

Eternity is the final destination; but in the meantime, let's treasure the time we have on earth.

PRAYER PROMPT

Heavenly Father, thank you for the gift of life. You didn't have to create me, yet out of the abundance of your love, you made me so I can enjoy my time and find fulfillment in You. Help me take advantage of youth and age well, embracing life today while keeping the end in mind. In Jesus' Name, Amen.

---

[9] Christ Centered

Day 20
THERE MAY NOT ALWAYS BE TOMORROW

READ: Ecclesiastes 12: 1-8

> [1] *Remember your Creator*
> *in the days of your youth,*
> *before the days of trouble come*
> *and the years approach when you will say,*
> *"I find no pleasure in them"—*
>
> [2] *before the sun and the light*
> *and the moon and the stars grow dark,*
> *and the clouds return after the rain;*
>
> [3] *when the keepers of the house tremble,*
> *and the strong men stoop,*
> *when the grinders cease because they are few,*
> *and those looking through the windows grow dim;*
>
> [4] *when the doors to the street are closed*
> *and the sound of grinding fades;*
> *when people rise up at the sound of birds,*
> *but all their songs grow faint;*
>
> [5] *when people are afraid of heights*
> *and of dangers in the streets;*
> *when the almond tree blossoms*

THERE MAY NOT ALWAYS BE TOMORROW

*and the grasshopper drags itself along
and desire no longer is stirred.
Then people go to their eternal home
and mourners go about the streets.*

*⁶ Remember him—before the silver cord is severed,
and the golden bowl is broken;
before the pitcher is shattered at the spring,
and the wheel broken at the well,*

*⁷ and the dust returns to the ground it came from,
and the spirit returns to God who gave it.*

*⁸ "Meaningless! Meaningless!" says the Teacher
"Everything is meaningless!"*

I moved to Montreal a week after graduating from college. Like many decisions made during that time, it was quick and void of prayer or spiritual guidance. Goal number one: GET AWAY. Away from what, exactly? I was not quite sure. But I knew, in all my infinite wisdom gained during my twenty-one years, that I was tired of people (most notably my parents) telling me how to live. Running away was not a new strategy of mine. I ran away to college, to Scotland, and then to Montreal. In all three places, God dealt with my heart. He saw me, knew me, and wanted me to abide in Him no matter where I landed, a notion I continually pushed aside.

Submitting to God translated to me as living devoid of pleasure. Christianity seemed like a laundry list of rules that held me back. Ironically, while avoiding a "suppressive" relationship with God, I increasingly felt more depressed and alone in the world. It was exhausting pretending that everything was okay. The good news was that my parents and friends were thousands of miles away, so I was accountable to no one. All this "freedom" ultimately led to a full-blown breakdown that had me sobbing in my boss's office, packing my bags, and arriving home—back to my parent's house. I couldn't outrun God. He chose me to be His daughter and pursued me until I responded to His call of loving grace. No matter how hard I tried to push Him away, the Lord relentlessly pursued me. I just needed to surrender.

WHAT DOES IT MEAN?

As we near the end of Ecclesiastes, Solomon transitions from a tone of suggestion to a sense of urgency, "Listen up, this is important, take notes!" he exclaims. Chapter eleven's message once again repeats the overall theme of Ecclesiastes: enjoy the gift of life today but live with the end in mind. Solomon has spent a significant portion of the book encouraging us to remember that one day, we will die, face judgment for the deeds done in this life, and reside for all eternity with the Lord or be separated from His presence. Solomon reiterates that while we don't know all the details of the afterlife, contrary to what many believe, it's not just lights out. Remembering the brevity of life and embracing the uncertainty of when our life will end, should move us to action, instead of driving us to fear.

God is the Creator. We are created. We belong to Him. Our freedom and our salvation was bought at a price (1 Corinthians 6:20). The earlier in life we accept that our destinies are not ours but God's, the more peaceful, purposeful, and plentiful our lives will be. The first part of chapter twelve shares the effects of aging and gives us vivid images of death. From dust we were created, dust we will return (12:7). We must turn to God while we still have the chance. Don't believe the lie that you will always have tomorrow. While you have your youth, your health, and the ability to work and exist on this earth, embrace God's commandments and live a life that is pleasing to Him. This is Solomon's final attempt to remind his readers that no one can escape the curse of death. With the uncertainty of life, take no chances and turn to God now![10]

WHY DOES IT MATTER?

It's not uncommon for me to speak with a fellow believer, and during our conversation, they share a season of waywardness in their youth. Many people experience a time of rebellion, but after they have children, they eventually return to the Church. However, forgetting God doesn't just happen in our teens and twenties. It is easy to neglect our Creator when we are in the thick of life, the weeds of motherhood, high on the ladder of success, or in the trenches of caregiving. Corrie TenBoom is quoted saying, "If the devil can't make us bad, he'll make us busy." Ain't that the truth?

Solomon knew how easy it was to get distracted from God. Not only from personal experience, but Solomon was a product of his father David's sin (2 Samuel 11). David, a man after God's own heart, slept with another man's wife. The woman, named Bathsheba, became pregnant and lost the baby. As if all of that wasn't enough, David had her husband killed so that he could have her all to himself. Solomon was the second child of David and Bathsheba. They were married when they conceived Solomon, but their relationship was not in alignment with God's will. Following suit in similar marital

---

[10] *Akin, D., & Akin PhD., J. (2016). Exalting Jesus in Ecclesiastes (Christ-Centered Exposition Commentary). Holman Reference.*

dysfunction, Solomon had over 1000 wives and concubines (1 Kings 11:3), many of whom worshiped foreign gods and often led Solomon to stray from his faith. How did the wisest man in history make so many poor choices? Sin.

We are all affected by the consequences of sin. Less, we think too highly of ourselves, let's remember we can all fall victim to distraction, make bad decisions, and choose our way instead of the Lord's. While our rebellion has consequences, for those of us in Christ, we can never be separated from the love of God (Romans 8:38-39). Living under the authority of the Lord, keeping his commandments, and maintaining a biblical and eternal perspective won't always be easy, but it is always beneficial. As already discussed, time is short. There may not always be a tomorrow. Let's surrender to the Lord today!

THE HARD HEART WORK

We've discussed looking at our calendars and bank accounts to show what we value, but what about our hearts? We've become a society that is good at only showing our highlight reels, faking sincerity, and saving face when our hearts are far from God.

Meditate on this verse, *"Not everyone who calls out to me, 'Lord! Lord!' will enter the Kingdom of Heaven. Only those who actually do the will of my Father in heaven will enter. On judgment day many will say to me, 'Lord! Lord! We prophesied in your name and cast out demons in your name and performed many miracles in your name.' But I will reply, 'I never knew you. Get away from me, you who break God's laws"* (Matthew 7:21-23, NLT).

THERE MAY NOT ALWAYS BE TOMORROW

Are you a true disciple of Christ, or are you only going through the motions?

Have you accepted Christ as Savior but have yet to fully surrender and submit every detail of your life to Him?

If the Lord is revealing to you that you've strayed from His purpose for your life, what steps can you take to align the Lord's desires with your own?

For those who have accepted Christ as Savior, we must now surrender to God as Sovereign.

PRAYER PROMPT

Heavenly Father, I am often guilty of coming to you out of obligation instead of gratitude. Give me a heart open to receiving your instruction and bend my will to align with Yours. When I stray, bring me back to You. In Jesus' Name, Amen.

Day 21
HOW TO NOT WASTE YOUR LIFE

READ: Ecclesiastes 12:9-14

> *⁹ Not only was the Teacher wise, but he also imparted knowledge to the people. He pondered and searched out and set in order many proverbs. ¹⁰ The Teacher searched to find just the right words, and what he wrote was upright and true.*
>
> *¹¹ The words of the wise are like goads, their collected sayings like firmly embedded nails—given by one shepherd. ¹² Be warned, my son, of anything in addition to them.*
>
> *Of making many books there is no end, and much study wearies the body.*
>
> *¹³ Now all has been heard;*
> *here is the conclusion of the matter:*
> *Fear God and keep his commandments,*
> *for this is the duty of all mankind.*
>
> *¹⁴ For God will bring every deed into judgment,*
> *including every hidden thing,*
> *whether it is good or evil.*

I've always been an overachiever. If there was a task to be slayed, a gold star to be earned, or a need to be met, I was your gal. Unfortunately, this mentality made its way into my faith. I knew I was saved through faith alone and my redemption was a gift of grace from the Lord. However, I tirelessly felt the need to earn or prove my salvation for years. Out of obligation and fear of disappointing the Lord, I took on more than I should at the expense of my family and personal health, leaving me spiritually weary.

I am not sure why I have found it so hard to believe I don't have to earn God's love, that He delights in me for who I am. It's been a journey learning to choose joyful obedience over performance obligation, choosing to wait on the Lord over proving what I can do, and resting in Him over striving to gain approval. The gospel message isn't just for salvation. The Good News is we are redeemed and restored every day. It is a truth I preach to myself daily. Accept grace for yourself and others. Discover the freedom gained by knowing you are not enough, but you are made whole in Christ.

WHAT DOES IT MEAN?

If Solomon were a modern-day preacher, he would tell his congregation, "If you only remember one thing, remember this: fear God and keep His commandments" (insert mic drop). I am so glad you spent 21 days reading through Ecclesiastes, but if you only read Ecclesiastes 1:1-2 and 12:13, you would walk away with Solomon's primary message. A life lived without God will never satisfy you. You were created for a purpose. Enjoy the breath in your lungs today, fear God, and walk in obedience to His commands because one day, you will die and face eternal judgment.

Solomon wasn't just a sage teacher, he desired to use his knowledge to help others grow in wisdom and improve their lives today and for eternity. He didn't just randomly throw out his thoughts on paper. Instead, he carefully sought the best way to speak to his audience. These words should be cherished as tools to guide us as we thrive instead of merely surviving this life. Solomon's words are meant to guide and support us as we follow our Good Shepherd on the path He has ordained for us.

Solomon gives his son, who is about to take over the kingdom, a final warning about trying to find meaning outside of God. Solomon says, "I've tried it all; learn from my mistakes!" We were created for one purpose: to glorify God. There will be so many things in this life we can't understand, but we can rest in the hope that one day, God, the final judge, will bring every deed done under the sun into the light. We will all stand before God at the end of our lives and face eternal judgment. And one day, when Jesus returns, those of us in Christ will live in the new Heaven and new Earth, in the absence of sin and the presence of the Lord (Revelation 22:6-21).

WHY DOES IT MATTER?

Solomon's original audience didn't have the luxury of the Bible like we do today, something that I pray we never take for granted. As Solomon wraps up his speech and imparts final wisdom, he warns of potential consequences when looking outside his words (and for us today, the Bible) to find truth. We don't need to add or subtract God's Word. What was written down is the exact information we need to live a godly life. That is not to say that we don't enjoy reading books by other Christian authors. We can and should. But, only the

Bible is inerrant, infallible, and should be the only undeniable source of truth.

The Christian life really is simple. We make it more complicated than it should be. We spend so much time trying to "reinvent the wheel" and figure it all out. Jesus came so that we could have freedom from sin. It is by grace alone, through faith alone. There is nothing we have to earn or prove outside of the work of Jesus Christ on the cross—the free gift to us of salvation. All we have to do is accept.

Yet, we want to add it to it. We think there must be more. It must be Jesus and works. Jesus and saying yes to all the service opportunities. Jesus and reading our Bible. Jesus and filling in the blank to anything we've convinced ourselves will put us in a right standing before God. But these efforts to secure our own redemption are all in vain. It's only Jesus. We don't have to earn, hustle, strive, claw, and climb our way to our Savior. He tells us, "Come to me all who are weary, and I will give you rest" (Matthew 1:28-30).

THE HARD HEART WORK

Ephesians 2:8-9 tells us, "For it is by grace you have been saved, through faith—and this is not from yourselves, it is the gift of God—not by works so that no one can boast."

Above, we talked about how prone we are to add our terms to salvation. What areas in your life do you falsely believe will help secure your right standing before the Lord?

How does knowing God has a plan for your life free you from figuring out your next step or proving your self-worth?

Embracing Eternity IN THE HERE AND NOW

God gave us breath in our lungs and earthly possessions for pleasure and enjoyment, but all will be meaningless if we don't have a personal relationship with the Lord. Have you accepted Christ as Savior? If so, have you completely surrendered to Him as the Lord of your life?"

The keys to a life lived well are to love the Lord with all your heart, soul, and mind and keep His commandments.

PRAYER PROMPT

Heavenly Father, in a world of distraction, help me keep my focus on living for You. Stir my heart to seek You. Give me an appetite to read and study Your Word. May I delight in living for Your glory. Daily, help me take up our cross and follow You. In Jesus' Name, Amen.

EVERY DAY,
WE HAVE A CHOICE:

LIVE FOR

This World

OR

The Next.

Eternal WANDERLUST

> "He has made everything beautiful in its time.
> He has also set eternity in the human heart; yet, no one can fathom what God has done from beginning to end."
> Ecclesiastes 3:11

In several devotional entries, I referenced my struggle with submission to the Lord. One entry specifically described a moment when I boldly faced the reality that I could no longer outrun God. It was one of the darkest periods of my life. I find it painful to even think back to that time in Montreal. I remember one morning, I woke up on my closet floor. I'd been looking for shoes, but the thought of getting back up overwhelmed me, so I just lay there immobile.

How did it all become so intolerable that I felt the need to take refuge from my inner turmoil in a closet?

I needed help and to return home; this wasn't the life I was meant to be living.

Embracing Eternity IN THE HERE AND NOW

I eventually made my way back down South. My brother offered me a place to stay while I got back on my feet. Life was outwardly better, but inside, I still felt unsettled.

I was jobless, single, and living in my brother's guest room—the prodigal sister—not exactly the life I'd planned.

My brother graciously reminded me that my visit didn't come with an expiration date. I could have unpacked in an attempt to settle into my new "home," but placing my things in drawers and personalizing the room symbolized permanence.

This was only a short-term stop, not my final destination.

Eventually, I jumped back into the workforce, married, and moved into what my husband calls our "forever house." This move meant permanent residence. Drawers and cabinets now hold all of my personal possessions, and family photos hang on walls painted in colors chosen by me. Yet, I still wrestle with wanderlust, a feeling that this house isn't really my home.

Today, I am surrounded by a loving, godly, supportive family, church community, friends, co-workers, and neighbors. My faith remains solid while I continue to "work out my salvation" (Philippians 2:12). The Lord continues to sanctify me, grant grace, extend patience and forgiveness, and show me His mercy and love daily.

And yet, my soul still feels unsettled. Not like that time in Montreal or in my late twenties before I fully surrendered my life to Christ, but I still sense that something isn't quite right. I am not entirely settled.

Ecclesiastes 3:11 says, *"He has made everything beautiful in its time. He has also set eternity in the human heart; yet, no one can fathom what God has done from beginning to end."*

ETERNAL WANDERLUST

My sense of restlessness accurately represents the status of our humanity. We were made for eternity to dwell in the House of the Lord, to be in the presence of our Creator. Those of us who are new creations in Christ have been justified; we continue to be sanctified, and one day we will be glorified! We are experiencing the full weight of God's "already and not yet" kingdom.

So while we patiently endure this temporal existence, let us wait well. Enjoy the blessings provided for us through a loving and gracious God. Find pleasure in life. Eat, drink, and be merry! Take delight in your days under the sun. But hold it all loosely; everything in the here and now will one day cease to exist. Don't allow the lesser things to distract you from the greater goodness and riches found in Christ.

Ecclesiastes can be difficult to read, so, friend, I am glad you stuck with it. Well done! You've finished! I hope you now have a new adoration (if not, then at least appreciation), for this book that is, as we say today, filled with truth bombs.

Within these pages, I've shared a significant part of my story, and you've had the opportunity to delve into Solomon's life, experiences, and lessons. I believe… no, I know, these words offer me immense comfort because I can relate to Solomon and his quest for meaning. I trust you, too, have found solace in this shared journey.

I pray that as you embrace an eternal perspective it will guide you to live a more peaceful, purposeful, and plentiful life today.

ONCE WE'VE ACCEPTED CHRIST AS *Savior,*

WE MUST NOW SURRENDER TO GOD AS *Sovereign.*

About
THE AUTHOR

Laura Bailey is an author and Bible teacher who encourages women to live with an eternal perspective. She helps them understand what they believe, why it's important, and how to live out their faith daily. She has written multiple books and Bible studies and regularly contributes to Proverbs 31 Ministries, Guideposts, Crosswalk, iBelieve Truth—Crosswalk, and Her View From Home.

Laura lives in Gaffney, SC, with her husband and three young girls, where she serves as director of women's ministries at her church. She loves long conversation-filled walks, reading on a rainy day with a cup of strong coffee, and has a deep affection for stationary and sending snail mail.

TRUE WORSHIP STEMS FROM INNER HEART *Transformation* THAT LEADS TO OUTWARD *Materialization.*

Teaching MINISTRY

While Laura loves the power of the written word, she is passionate about teaching and studying the Scriptures with other women. Laura welcomes the opportunity to speak at events of any size and to women of diverse backgrounds and multi-generational audiences. She would love the opportunity to partner with your church, women's leader, or sister in Christ who is looking to invite someone to speak at their event.

While Laura is grateful for any opportunity to teach God's Word, retreats and multi-session conferences is where she thrives. Having the chance to look deeper into Scripture, engage with attendees, and spend time in fellowship is simply the best!

To request Laura to speak or learn more about her ministry, scan below:

THE GOSPEL MESSAGE ISN'T JUST FOR *Salvation.*

THE GOOD NEWS IS WE ARE *Redeemed* AND *Restored* EVERY DAY.

Connect
WITH LAURA

(scan QR Codes to be directed to links)

WEBSITE

www.LauraRBailey.com

AMAZON AUTHOR'S PAGE
{Follow to be notified of Laura's new releases and browse past titles}

Facebook: LauraBaileyWrites
Instagram: LauraBaileyWrites
Email: LauraBaileyWrites@LauraRBailey.com

Made in the USA
Columbia, SC
01 August 2025

bce4ffa5-5345-4f1d-8335-a78da002d761R01